The Oglala Sioux chief, Iron Tail (Sinte Maza), photographed while working with the 101 Ranch. Born on the North American Plains in the mid-nineteenth century, he saw many changes in the lifestyle of his people, as this photograph poignantly illustrates.

Cover: Detail of a beaded bag, recycled from a Teton Sioux tobacco bag, circa 1890.

Author's collection.

The Only Handsome Woman (Blackfoot), wife of Dog Child. Photograph by Trueman & Caple (National Archives of Canada, PA-195224).

A Warrior I Have Been

Plains Indian Cultures in Transition

The Richard Green Collection of Plains Indian Art

Text by Richard Green

With an Introduction by Michael G. Johnson

A warrior
I have been.
Now it is all over.
A hard time
I have.
—Song of Sitting Bull

Dedicated to the memory of *Winyan Waśte Win* (1915-2003)

A Warrior I Have Been

Plains Indian Cultures in Transition

The Richard Green Collection of Plains Indian Art

Written Heritage
PO Box 1390
Folsom, LA 70437-1390
(985) 796-5433
1-800-301-8009
www.writtenheritage.com

Contents

Acknowledgments

The author would like to thank the following individuals for their invaluable help in the preparation of this book:

Alan Hughes, Michael G. Johnson, Dr Carole Morris, Alan C. Mitchell, Moose and Lizzie Wells, Tony Prout, Frank Bergevin and Mussarrat Gill, for their support, encouragement and friendship; Professor Bill Holm, Benson Lanford, Dr Hugh Dempsey, Rory Sumner, Dr Colin Taylor and Mike Kostelnik, for kindly giving the benefit of their knowledge regarding individual catalog items; David B. Bailey, Anna Meredith, Alan Giles, Tom F. Cunningham, Nico Strange Owl, Darlene C. Heriard, Alan Gallop, Walt Marsh and Jonathan Smith, for their generosity and practical support; and finally Jack B. Heriard of Written Heritage, Inc., for his patience and advice throughout this project. Any inaccuracies, however, remain wholly the responsibility of the author.

Unless otherwise credited, all images and artifacts illustrated in this publication are from the author's private collection and archive.

Foreword

I am extremely honored to be writing the foreword for a book which now allows much of the author's lifetime work in studying and collecting the material culture of Plains Indian tribal groups to be shared with the public. This book will form a permanent visual and textual record of the Plains material from the Richard Green Collection. The artifacts are magnificent—sometimes simple, often complex, using evocative, beautiful and intricate patterns to decorate weapons, clothing, special regalia, everyday items and even items for sale.

Richard has been working to achieve a major exhibition of Plains tribal material for several years, and *A Warrior I Have Been*, which will run at the Birmingham Museum and Art Gallery from 17 July to 5 September 2004, is the culmination of this endeavor.

The exhibition aims to trace the evolution of Plains Indian art and culture from early times to the present day, including material from a wide range of tribal groups. Represented in the exhibition are many items from Richard's own collection, as well as others from the BM&AG collections and from other British museums.

The initial part of the book consists of five authoritative and empathetic essays on themes relating both to the transition and change evident in Plains Indian cultures in the late nineteenth and early twentieth centuries, and the interesting theme of stereotypes of Plains Indians.

In both Chapter 1, *Behold These Things - Northern Plains Men's Parade Regalia* and Chapter 2, *Something Splendid I Wear – Plains Women's Trade Cloth Dresses,* Richard presents his thoughts on Plains clothing where the emphasis is on the revolution in Plains material culture brought about both as a result of imported trade materials such as glass beads and woven cloth, and of the tragic end of traditional buffalo hunting culture and subsequent confinement on government reservations.

Chapter 3, *In Paint and Feathers – On Tour with Pahaska*, narrates the visit to Birmingham by Buffalo Bill Cody and his Sioux recruits in 1903, and the powerful effect it had on the people of the city at the time. Cody's visits fed into (and altered) existing stereotypes of Native American peoples, previously derived from literature about the Great Lakes tribes—J. Fenimore Cooper's *Last of the Mohicans*, Longfellow's *Song of Hiawatha*, etc. For the first time, the emphasis of stereotypes focused on Plains peoples.

Chapter 4, *Some Honor I Seek – Sioux Indians in Early Postcards*, analyses the way in which Sioux Indians became popular subjects for picture postcards in the Edwardian era and just after, and presents over seventy magnificent illustrations from Richard's photographic archive.

Chapter 5, *White Man's Vision – Evolving Stereotypes of the Plains Indian*, deals with the ever-changing issue of stereotypes of Plains Indians, including the eternal fondness for the 'feather warbonnet' and the discrepancy between the idea of the 'Noble Savage' (modern-day environmentalist) versus that of the 'bloodthirsty barbarian', as portrayed in countless Hollywood western movies.

The second part of this book catalogs the Richard Green Collection of Plains material, much of which formed part of the BM&AG exhibition. As such, it is the first published catalog of a British private collection of this kind, and includes fine examples of Plains beadwork, quillwork, featherwork, footwear, dance regalia, horsegear, items relating to childhood, etc. The items have been collected over a period of about twenty-five years. Over 150 objects are described and illustrated in the 'Catalog' section, each with details of the object's function, area of origin, date, constituent materials and dimensions. The *Warrior's World* has sections on weapons, trade cloth clothing, non-native influences and dance regalia. *The Woman's World* includes tools, utensils, containers and clothing. Further sections divide into childhood, horsegear, moccasins, bags and pouches, and items made for sale.

Both this catalog and the exhibition are seminal in representing a rather 'British' angle on Native American cultures. They reflect reactions to Sioux Indians visiting Britain with W.F. Cody. They remind us that large quantities of trade materials (woolen and cotton textiles, metal trade goods, including Sheffield steel blades, needles, and even beads) were manufactured in our industrial cities. The catalog is that of a British private collection, and it was exhibited in Birmingham, England. May the book remain a standard reference volume for many years to come!

Dr Carole Morris
Cambridge, England
February 2004

Introduction

Michael G. Johnson

We all have mental images of different peoples, some grounded in fact, some positive, some wholly inaccurate. White Europeans and Americans often have powerful images of the original inhabitants of the North American Plains, variously gleaned from reports of European explorers, adventure writers, or the paintings of artist-travelers such as Karl Bodmer and George Catlin who, in the 1830s, portrayed Indian life west of the Mississippi River in its pristine grandeur. Later images were derived first-hand from traveling 'Wild West' shows such as that of William F. Cody, popularly known as Buffalo Bill—and then later still from western films of the twentieth century.

Visitors to the exhibition, which accompanies this catalog, are invited to re-examine their own perceptions and visual images with a review of the material culture and art objects on display which, by and large, were made by native women during the period of great transition and change following the collapse of their culture, food supply and forced confinement on government reservations (or reserves in Canada) during the late nineteenth century.

American Indians are a people of Asiatic origin who crossed to the New World via the Bering Strait, Alaska, starting perhaps 15,000 years ago and who, in time, occupied the whole of the Americas, both north and south. The Great Plains of North America range between the Missouri River and the Rocky Mountains and stretch from the Mexican border to the Parklands of western Canada. The area was thinly populated by migratory bands, and maize farmers living at the margins of this vast area. Beginning in the late seventeenth century, a dynamic revised culture developed as a result of the merging of two phenomena. First was the native domestication of the horse, brought to the Americas by the Spanish Conquistadors; and secondly, pressure on tribal groups in newly colonized eastern North America to move west in promotion of the fur trade. Greater mobility provided by the horse and later the acquisition of firearms, allowed a dozen or more tribal groups to harvest the abundance of bison (American buffalo) which roamed the Plains in vast herds.

The material wealth of these new arrivals was increasingly augmented by the availability of European trade goods, such as guns, knives, iron tomahawks, beads, and loomed trade cloth before the close of the eighteenth century. In this nomadic world, male warrior fraternities thrived, initiating dangerous inter-tribal warfare and horse raiding. Their religious complexes recognized and placated the natural climatic forces, and their ceremonial cycle of dramatic displays of dances mimicked animal characteristics and warrior exploits. Religious power was recorded and revealed in the painting and decoration of ceremonial accoutrements such as robes and tipi covers with linear or realistic symbolism.

Animal skin clothing was adorned with porcupine quills, bird quills, plant fiber or trade beads in conspicuously colorful and reflective areas, often in conjunction with blue or red trade cloth. Increasingly, mosaics of sewn beadwork, employing imported glass trade beads in a wide range of colors, became popular after about 1860.

Some semi-agricultural eastern tribes have a tradition of using quartz crystals, shiny native copper plates and shells to harness the reflective spiritual power of the sun's rays. In similar tradition, Plains people used trade beads, brass buttons, tin cones and mirrors, obtained from white traders, to emphasize the dazzle of reflected light from ceremonial dress, no doubt heightened in the clear, dry and bright High Plains atmosphere.

In the north, Indians and emerging mixed-bloods, the natural result of the fur trade, absorbed floral imagery of European flavor into their indigenous curvilinear traditions, giving a hybrid feel to much late nineteenth century decorative regalia, a legacy of the more positive interaction between the races. In the second half of the nineteenth century, however, the Plains Indians were pushed aside by Euro-American settlement, assigned to reservations and subjected to harsh treatment by government agents who restricted religious ceremonials and native dress and suppressed the use of native language. Their population, perhaps never numbering more than 130,000, was halved by disease and starvation during this period, a fact which still sits uncomfortably with us. However, it was a period when women, perhaps freed from the labors of nomadic camp life, had time to facilitate considerable quantities of beadwork which they produced for trade and sale as well as for indigenous use.

For men, inactive reservation life was restrictive and dull, with native rituals limited to the American festive calendar such as the fourth of July celebrations, becoming more secular with warriors' accoutrements, such as modified shields, clubs, banners and tomahawks, now used as male dancers' accessories. A number of men eagerly joined the wild west shows which toured the eastern states and Europe, presenting sham battles and war dances to cheering audiences. Such displays, and the increased interaction between different tribes, was a preliminary ingredient of the now ubiquitous pow wow, a recent phenomenon and a continuing expression of Indian art, dress, song and dance across all of Indian North America today.

We cannot bring back to life the warriors and their folk who paraded through the streets of Birmingham, or pitched their tipis on the open grounds in Aston Lane, Birmingham, during Buffalo Bill's touring show, a hundred years ago. But we can marvel at the splendor of their contemporary clothing and accoutrements.

The exhibition, *A Warrior I Have Been*, consists largely of the private collection of Richard Green, whose life has been dedicated to the understanding and study of Native Americans and their material culture. It is a tribute to the Plains people whose story these objects tell, and also to Richard himself, fortuitously a member of staff of Birmingham Museums & Art Gallery, who have graciously provided the means and support to hold the exhibition, together with generous support from other British institutions

You are now invited to take away perhaps different images and impressions of Native American society.

A group of warriors, including the famed Chiricahua Apache chief, Geronimo, posing incongruously in a motor car.

Behold These Things
Northern Plains Men's Parade Regalia

By the 1890s, many of the traditional warrior societies of the Plains peoples had disappeared. Enforced assimilation and change in Plains Indian cultures had never been greater than at this time.

On the reservations, log houses were replacing tipis. Indians queued to receive weekly government food rations, distributed by the Indian agencies. Poor diet and living conditions led to a generally low standard of health among many Plains peoples. Native religious practices were outlawed and missionaries encouraged conversion to Christianity.

Throughout this transitional period, the process of adaptation and cultural change was a painful one for these once nomadic warrior peoples. In an effort to maintain some vestige of traditional practices, certain Northern Plains peoples established annual horse parades and traditional dances. These events steadily gained in popularity throughout the first half of the twentieth century, and soon became a popular attraction for visitors to the Canadian Rockies. Celebrations such as Banff Indian Days and Calgary Stampede became a focus for Indian heritage, attended by tribes from the various local reserves.

A real revolution had taken place in Northern Plains men's traditional regalia since the buffalo hunting days came to an end in the second half of the nineteenth century. By 1900, numerous new styles of ceremonial clothing and horse regalia were becoming fashionable among the Blackfoot, Stoney-Assiniboines, Sarsi and Plains Cree.

A wealth of contemporary photographs and commercially produced postcards document the early parade days at Banff and Calgary, including studio portraits and views of mounted Northern Plains horsemen in their magnificent regalia. One of the most noteworthy of photographers of Indian subjects in the Rocky Mountains region was Byron Harmon, who was based in Banff from 1903 until the early 1930s. Careful study of these images reveals fascinating details of the new styles of clothing, horsegear and accessories used by these strikingly dressed warriors.

Although tribal styles varied somewhat from one group to another in the Canadian provinces of Alberta and Saskatchewan, several of the indigenous nations in the vicinity of the Rockies shared a similar range of chiefs' clothing, horse trappings and other paraphernalia. Much of this material was made as a direct result of Blackfoot and Plains Cree influence, these groups being among the most influential in the region.

Articles of clothing include magnificently decorated buckskin shirts and leggings, beaded moccasins, panel belts, loop necklaces, and vests. Horse regalia comprises ornately beaded martingales, cruppers, saddle cloths, and headstalls.

Beadwork decoration consisted either of bold geometric design units, or sometimes stylized floral compositions, almost invariably in the couched overlay technique. In the late nineteenth century, the Stoneys shared the typical Blackfoot repertoire of geometric designs composed of small square or rectangular blocks, and straight-sided hourglasses with small-scale projections at each end. By the early twentieth century, they favored bolder geometric designs such as chevrons, crosses and 8-pointed star motifs, often on strikingly colored backgrounds, bright red being typical. Indeed, among most Canadian Plains groups, Czech beads took over from Venetian stock after World War I. The Stoneys also liked to use a variety of French sparkling and metallic effect glass beads with faceted sides.

Chiefs' Suits

Shirts became increasingly tailored in cut after the turn of the century. They were made of creamy white brain-tanned buckskin or elk hide, and the fashion during this period was for matching leggings to complete the beaded ensemble. These outfits with matching beadwork are sometimes referred to as 'chiefs' suits'. Wide beaded strips ran down sleeves and across the shoulders, and a V-shaped bib was the norm to both back and front. Beadwork designs tended towards bold geometric units, often composed of small squares or rectangles, as previously described. Repeated diagonal bands of such blocks were a popular choice, usually on a background of white or blue beads. Several later Stoney examples, in particular, employed backgrounds of bright red, royal blue, green, orange and yellow.

Beadwork was generally commercial thread-sewn and couched. Seams on clothing were often sinew-sewn. Shirts were heavily fringed at the arms, sometimes with ermine skin pendants. The edges of garments were often decoratively serrated, castellated or scalloped. Necklines of shirts were typically folded over, stitched down, and similarly cut. The lower edge of shirts, and the cuffs of sleeves, were sometimes broadly cut into 'swallowtail' fringes, often pierced with holes for added decoration. This was a survival of a nineteenth century form of shirt and legging decoration. (See Stoney shirt illustrated on page 90).

Buckskin leggings, from the early twentieth century onwards, were of the 'chap' type, predominantly square-cut, with wide beaded couched overlay strips, often matching those on the shirt. Each legging was closed using a series of buckskin laces, tied at front or back. The outer edges of the flaps received similar decoratively cut treatment, or were left plain. (See page 91).

A late style of buckskin suit, particularly popular from the 1930s onwards, consisted of a tailored shirt, often open at the front, with collar, pockets, and tailored cuffs. They had fringed sleeves and fitted cuffs. The pockets were decorated with stylized floral beadwork. The shirt was accompanied by matching leggings, also with pockets, with rounded 'chaps' and floral beadwork.

Vests

When the full white buckskin suit was not worn, a fully-beaded vest with bold geometric, or sometimes floral, designs was a popular alternative, worn over a plain or patterned cotton shirt. Canvas quickly replaced buckskin as a substrate for large areas of beadwork. Typical Stoney taste often consisted of stacked arrangements of hourglasses, rectangles or diamonds, with diagonal devices made up of small rectangular blocks positioned at the shoulders; and rows of small-scale diamonds to the lower edge of the composition. (See pages 103 and 104). Vests usually had plain cloth backs, and tended to be lined with patterned cotton cloth.

Gloves and Cuffs

Gauntlet type gloves with fully-beaded cuffs decorated with bold geometric or floral designs in couched overlay were sometimes worn, even in combination with white buckskin suits. (See pages 14, 24, 25). Alternatively, large-sized beaded cuffs with similar decoration were popular throughout the twentieth century. (See page 13).

Headgear

The crowning glory of Northern Plains parade regalia was the eagle feather warbonnet, of Sioux flaring style, often of the double trailer type. Stoney bonnets were particularly ornate in style, sometimes decorated with Blackfoot style pericardium banded or spiraled 'crackers' and brightly colored fluffy feathers at the base of each eagle tail feather. In the case of trailer bonnets, the cloth trailer section was often split or unusually shaped, and decoration thereupon took the form of multicolored ribbon edgings, sequins, dyed feathers, and cut cloth applique work.

Another type of bonnet favored by the Northern Plains groups is the split-horn bonnet, the cap of which was shingled with scraps of ermine fur and full ermine pelts. The use of this type of bonnet has a long history among several of the Northern Plains groups.

Horsegear

The martingale, a survival from the nineteenth century, was used by many Northern Plains parade riders. Its function was originally to prevent the horse from throwing back its head, although later examples were a purely decorative addition to parade regalia. Some examples appear to be simple straps of harness leather, decorated with sleigh bells. The more ornate twentieth century variants were of two basic types—the first was similar to the Crow and Plateau type, comprising a rectangular or shaped canvas panel, attached between two vertical strips, usually fully beaded with bold beadwork designs. The second, the type generally used by women in conjunction with a decorated crupper, was constructed of an elongated band of red, dark blue or black woolen trade cloth, decorated with stylized floral designs in couched overlay technique. Many examples have suspensions of trade beads and metal trade bells or brass thimbles. (See page 18, lower photo).

Cruppers, also originating in nineteenth century Plains equestrian material culture, continued to be made throughout the early twentieth century, used by women in combination with martingales. Earliest examples were decorated with geometric beadwork, but were later made of red, navy blue or black woolen trade cloth. They were made in two halves, connected at the lower end, the opposite ends tapering in, and the outer edges rounded off at the bottom. Decoration of typical twentieth century examples consisted of cut cloth appliqué work in contrasting colors, and stylized beadwork, often of a floral or semi-floral nature, within decorative borders.

Soft pad saddles, stuffed with animal hair, were traditionally used by Northern Plains men, while rigid saddles with high pommels tended to be used by women. These, however, are rarely visible in contemporary photographs as they were invariably concealed under masses of beaded parade regalia.

Elaborately decorated headstalls, sometimes with beaded neck panels and reins, were popular among the Alberta groups, and remain so today. (See page 24).

Parade horses were further decorated with saddle 'cloths', made of an entire tanned hide or of woolen cloth, and applied with a colorfully beaded band or an arrangement of panels with bold geometric or floral designs. Huge 'stoles'

This photograph, issued by the Coast Publishing Co, Vancouver, shows the celebrated Blackfoot chief, Duck Chief. Note the heavily beaded martingale with geometric designs, the blanket with wide beaded blanket strip, as well as his warbonnet and fine shirt and leggings with ermine skin trim. He holds a lance, spirally wrapped in colored cloth. Note also the feather-decorated medicine charm attached to the horse's bit, as well as the miniature shield painted with symbolic designs, hanging from the front of the saddle.

or blanket strips, often mounted onto woolen cloth blankets, were draped over the horse's hindquarters. (See page 19, top photo).

Other Accessories

Accessories carried by horsemen during parades include heavily fringed gun cases, parade lances, pipe-tomahawks and clubs with large triangular pendant drops, and tobacco bags, (sometimes matching the beadwork designs on the buckskin suit). Several groups favored bead-wrapped loop necklaces, often incorporating large glass or metal trade beads. Among the Stoney and the Blackfoot, beaded collar and necktie sets were popular in the 1920s and 30s, and are still worn by these groups to this day.

This dynamic of cultural adaptation has long been a feature of Plains Indian life. Responding to the stimulus of change to traditional lifestyle, including the revolutionary influence of imported trade materials, Plains peoples embraced what they deemed to be useful in the constant process of cultural redefinition and reinvention. This is perhaps the most impressive of survival skills of the North American indigenous peoples—their innate ability, often in the face of adversity, to re-interpret traditional values within the context of an ever-changing world. Far from being members of what was once described as a 'Vanishing Race', Native Americans continue to be a vital presence in modern, evolving North American society.

This studio portrait by Byron Harmon shows a Stoney man dressed for a parade, probably in the 1920s. He wears a flaring eagle feather bonnet, fringed with ermine, a large bead-wrapped loop necklace, and beaded vest over a dark cloth shirt. Note also his wide beaded armbands and cuffs, cloth leggings with panels of geometric beadwork, and side-seam moccasins with buckles at the ankles. His face is painted with lines and rows of dots.

Mark Poucette was one of a number of Stoneys associated with Banff Indian Days. In this studio photograph by Byron Harmon, probably dating from the 1920s, he appears as if dressed for a dance. He is wearing an ermine-trimmed split-horn bonnet, loop necklace of brass trade beads and bead-wrapped rolls, wide armbands and belt with geometric couched overlay beadwork, short breechcloth, and part-beaded moccasins with stylized floral designs. The well-made bow and two arrows may be photographer's props.

This Sarsi group is presumably dressed for a parade or some ceremonial occasion, probably in the 1930s. The two men are wearing fine shirts and leggings of white buckskin. The man in the center wears shirt and leggings with matching strips of couched overlay beadwork, and a U-shaped bib to front. The suit worn by the man on the left is trimmed with ermine pelts. He also wears a beaded panel belt and aprons made of patterned Pendleton style blanket cloth. The men's moccasins are of the Northern side-seam style. The woman, at right, is Maggie Big Belly, who wears a heavily beaded buckskin dress, decorated in lane-stitch technique.

This fine portrait by Byron Harmon shows a man, possibly Blackfoot, in eagle warbonnet with ermine pelt browband and further ermine pelts suspended from the sides. He wears a tailored shirt of white buckskin, the beaded strips decorated with geometric designs in couched overlay technique. A circular medallion adorns the center of the shirt, at chest level. Around his neck he wears a necklace of cowrie shells.

The unidentified subjects of this studio portrait wear an array of traditional Northern Plains finery. The man on the left wears a roach and woolen cloth shirt with beaded strips, triangular bib and buckskin fringe. His leggings are made of woolen cloth with undyed selvedge incorporating dark stripes, and have narrow beaded strips with a design of simple rectangular blocks. He displays an interesting dance ornament of peacock and stripped eagle secondary feathers, with a metal-rimmed trade mirror at the center. The man on the right, equally splendidly dressed, wears a beaded shirt, probably made some years before the date of the photograph, with beaded strips and long, fine buckskin fringe. His fur breastplate is adorned with metal-rimmed trade mirrors. His breechcloth consists of a short piece of double-stripe selvedge cloth over a longer section with ribbonwork decoration. In his left hand he holds some kind of fur dance ornament, heavily beaded and fringed, a bandoleer of brass trade beads, and what appears to be a slender forked stick of undetermined function. The hairstyles of both men, possibly Assiniboines or Plains Cree, are also rather unusual. The man on the right may be the same individual as the one depicted in the photograph on page 23.

This portrait of the famed Stoney chief, Hector Crawler, was taken by Byron Harmon in the 1920s or 30s. Note the wide flaring trailer bonnet with beaded browband, trimmed with brass bead suspensions and white ermine fur. His shirt is splendidly decorated with appliqué strips and ermine pelts. Note the low placement of the bib, visible below the beaded collar. This is a typical Stoney and Blackfoot trait in the 1920s. The cross design on the beaded collar reflects a Christian influence, many of the Stoneys having converted to Methodism by this period.

This portrait of Big Face Chief, Piegan, was taken by Harry Pollard. He is pictured wearing an ermine-trimmed horned bonnet, possibly with a single horn. His shirt is decorated with beaded strips and rectangular bib of woolen cloth, his braids wrapped in otter fur.

PIEGAN INDIAN CHIEF

INDIAN SHILDREN. 511

These two Northern Plains children wear exact copies of adult parade regalia. The boy wears a warbonnet and hide shirt and leggings with geometric beadwork decoration in couched overlay technique. Note the serrated cut edge to both the shirt and leggings. The ensemble is trimmed with brass bells, conch shell discs and ermine skins, and set off with beaded necktie, a broad belt, gloves and part-beaded moccasins. The young girl wears a cloth dress, the yoke of which is decorated with parallel rows of basket beads and dentalium shells, with heavily beaded belt and leggings.
The photograph is by Byron Harmon.

A handwritten inscription to the reverse of the photograph describes an Indian parade witnessed at Banff while the narrator was staying at the Banff Springs Hotel, probably in the 1920s:-

'There was a Grand Parade each morning, finishing off at this hotel with the distribution of prizes. On the second day we went to the sports and saw some wonderful bare back racing, wrestling on horseback, bow and arrow contest, pitching and striking the tepees, [and] various cowboy races. They are wonderfully at home on a horse, and their dress was most gorgeous.'

This interesting photograph, copyrighted by A.P.K. Co, shows a group of riders at the Calgary Stampede in 1912. Both men in the foreground wear white buckskin shirts, the shirt worn by the man on the left being ermine-trimmed. The man in the foreground wears a trailer warbonnet, and holds a riding quirt with brass tack decoration. A woman, on the left, partly concealed, rides a horse with heavily fringed crupper.

This photograph by Byron Harmon shows a group of Stoney women in ceremonial regalia at Banff in the 1920s or 30s. A tipi camp was regularly set up in the town for visitors to the Banff Indian Days event. The women's horses are decked out in a variety of horse trappings, including beaded martingales. The horse on the extreme left wears a beaded headstall, an unusual netted neck covering, and a Sioux style beaded saddle blanket. It was customary for women to wear men's warbonnets at such events.

A group of Stoneys at the tipi encampment at Banff in the 1920s or 30s photographed by Byron Harmon. The man on the left wears a white buckskin suit and beaded gauntlet type gloves. He carries a beaded and fringed gun case, and has a finely beaded woolen blanket draped over the hindquarters of his horse. The man in the center is Chief Sitting Eagle (John Hunter) of the Chiniki band at Morley Reserve. His wife is pictured on the right. All three wear immature golden eagle tail feather warbonnets in Sioux flaring style. Chief Sitting Eagle wears a matching white buckskin suit with bold geometric designs. There are several photographs of Sitting Eagle wearing this outfit. The beaded strips have a bright red background. The chief always held the utmost regard for Stoney traditions. His tipi, with painted 'eagle' design, appears at the left of the photograph.

This view by Byron Harmon records one of the early parades through Banff. The women in the middle of the procession wear sateen dresses with decorated yokes.

Another photograph by Byron Harmon, showing a Stoney couple outside their painted tipi, probably in the tipi village set up during Banff Indian Days. The man wears an otter fur breastplate with metal-framed trade mirrors, gauntlet type gloves with fully-beaded cuffs, and wool cloth leggings with beaded panels.

506. STONEY INDIAN AND SQUAW.

Photograph by Byron Harmon of John Salda, a Stoney, wearing an eagle feather bonnet and beautifully beaded vest with geometric couched overlay designs. Note that he wears his hair loose, and wears a cloth shirt beneath his vest. The vest, now in the collections of the Royal Ontario Museum, is strikingly similar to the example illustrated on page 103.

This photograph, published as a postcard around 1907 by W.G. MacFarlane of Toronto and Buffalo, shows a Piegan warrior in traditional regalia. He wears a beaded hide shirt of some vintage, the couched overlay strips featuring simple bands of color on a white background. Both the horned bonnet, heavily shingled in ermine pelts, and the breastplate made from a whole animal skin, relate to one of the Piegan warrior societies. The man holds the tail end of the breastplate, terminating in a cluster of hawk feathers, in his right hand.

BLACKFOOT INDIAN CHIEF.

The warbonnet worn by this Blackfoot chief has a quilled browband and large floral rosettes, possibly a later addition. The eagle feathers at the front are decorated with circular 'spots'. He also wears a choker of cowrie shells, bead-wrapped loop necklace, and plain fringed hide shirt.

This photograph by Mills, taken at Washed Oaks pow wow near Carlyle, shows a large crowd of onlookers watching dancing in progress. A group of singers, all wearing brimmed felt hats, is seated on the ground around a drum, to the right of the photograph. Most of the dancers wear finely beaded hide shirts. The man in the photograph on the opposite page, wearing a warbonnet of mature golden eagle tail feathers, appears at the center.

This photograph was taken at Washed Oaks pow wow near Carlyle, Saskatchewan in the 1920s. The father and son depicted are probably Plains Cree. Each wears a beaded hide shirt, eagle feather warbonnet, woolen cloth leggings, and carry a tomahawk. Large numbers of white spectators congregate in the background.

Another photograph issued as a postcard by W.G. MacFarlane, Toronto, showing two Stoney men in parade regalia. The man on the left wears a short hide shirt with beaded strips, the sleeves richly decorated with ermine pelts.

Hector Crawler, the Stoney chief, in his finest parade attire, including trailer warbonnet with split trailer of immature golden eagle tail feathers, matching buckskin shirt and leggings with bold geometric designs on a royal blue background, and heavily beaded gauntlet style gloves with floral designs. His horse is adorned with the full range of Stoney finery—fully-beaded martingale, heavily beaded headstall with neck embellishments, and a saddle throw. A wide beaded 'stole' with large circular medallions is also draped over the horse. He holds a parade lance wrapped in fur and decked with eagle tail feathers. The bold star motifs on the martingale collar are a typically Stoney choice of design. The photograph was taken in the 1930s. Hector Crawler was a familiar sight at local events such as Banff Indian Days and Calgary Stampede.

Blackfoot man in parade attire at Calgary, photographed by Dan McComan in 1926. The reverse of the photograph is marked – 'White Head Chief, Blackfoot tribe'. Of particular note is the beaded buckskin shirt with painted 'tadpole' designs to the sleeves, a characteristic of somewhat older Blackfoot shirts. Note also the splendid eagle feather warbonnet in Sioux style, with floral-beaded browband; the loop necklace with large conch shell discs; the large gloves with zoomorphic beadwork to the cuffs; and the floral-beaded strap over the wrist, presumably attached to a riding quirt.

Something Splendid I Wear
Plains Trade Cloth Dresses

The trend for decorating the yoke section of women's dresses with prestigious trade ornaments is long established. The earliest depictions of Plains women by artists like George Catlin and Karl Bodmer illustrate the value placed on such items as elk teeth and marine shells.

The attraction of hard-to-find decorative items to adorn traditional clothing is obvious. As highly desirable trade commodities, such items were an important form of currency to the Indian peoples of the Plains.

Elk teeth, the upper canines or milk teeth from the mature elk, were valued for their association with long life, as they remained when the rest of the beast had fallen into decay. Only two of these tushes are procured from a single elk, hence the great value with which they were traditionally endowed. It is said that a hundred of these teeth equaled the value of a good horse.

Cowrie and other marine shells were also traded from neighboring tribes from the warm waters of the Pacific coast and applied to the yoke section of hide dresses.

From early days of white contact, the availability of imported trade goods such as glass pony beads, brass buttons, and tin cone jingles, further broadened the possibilities for the adornment of early nineteenth century women's dresses. By the late nineteenth century, traders' stores were supplying Indians with a wide range of commercial goods. Diverse types of woolen and cotton cloth, European glass beads, as well as silk ribbon, brass bells, mirrors, metal thimbles and sequins were avidly sought after by Plains craft workers, and these new commodities quickly became incorporated into their traditional repertoire of materials.

With the availability of woolen trade cloth, an innovative style of dress became popular among Plains women in the nineteenth century. Although effectively cloth adaptations of binary 'deertail' skin dresses, the decorated trade cloth dress reflects a period of enormous transition and change in the lives of Plains peoples.

Commonly referred to as 'saved list' or 'broadcloth', the woolen cloth from which these dresses were made was manufactured in the northern English woolen mills, available in a range of colors, most commonly navy blue and scarlet red. Other colors, such as green and yellow, were also produced. Its most distinctive feature is the undyed white selvedge with a saw-tooth effect. This results from the curious production method in which, prior to dyeing, the outer edges of the cloth were folded by approximately half an inch and over-stitched for temporary reinforcement while the entire bolt of cloth was dyed in huge vats. The cloth was clamped tightly with toothed grips (sharp steel pins) along each edge, and suspended in the dyeing vat, the clamped edges positioned just above the level of the dye solution.

The resulting undyed white selvedge was, of course, merely a by-product of the dyeing process and not intentional. It was, however, of great aesthetic appeal to most Plains peoples, and was used to decorative effect on a range of apparel—not only women's dresses, but blankets, warbonnet trailers and men's leggings. Among the Sioux, it became the very hallmark of the 1890-1925 period, when large numbers of Sioux were recruited by touring wild west shows such as Buffalo Bill's Wild West and

Miller Brothers' 101 Ranch, displaying their traditional finery to audiences throughout the United States and Europe.

The construction of the trade cloth dress itself was very simple. A length of cloth was folded in half, the fold forming the shoulders of the dress, into which a transverse slit was made to form the neck. To this were added square-cut sleeves, stitched at right angles to the main section of the dress, forming a T-pattern. Tapered gussets were let into the side seams of the skirt section, these extending slightly below the hemline in imitation of the untrimmed legs on skin dresses.

Trade cloth dresses decorated with elk tushes were popular among a variety of Plains people, most notably the Crow. The tushes were applied to the yoke area of the dress in curved rows, as on hide dresses. Each tush was pierced with a single hole which then served as a means of attachment using thick cotton string or fine buckskin thong.

Even among the highest ranking of families, difficulty in obtaining sufficiently large numbers of elk teeth to fill an entire bodice led to the use of carefully carved imitations. These were usually carved of bone or elk antler, the appearance being given a little added authenticity by an application of brownish pigment to simulate tartar. Inspection of old elk tush dresses in museum collections reveals the extent of this crafty practice. Imitation elk teeth were available from trading posts in the late nineteenth and early twentieth centuries.

In addition to elk tush-decorated dresses, Plains women produced woolen cloth dresses with bodices decorated with rows of cowrie shells. These shells, long considered as a kind of trade currency by many Plains peoples, were drilled with a single hole and threaded onto the yoke using commercial cotton thread.

A further style of ornamented trade cloth dress was all the rage on the various Sioux reservations, particularly in South Dakota, at the turn of the nineteenth century. Its yoke section was solidly embellished with dentalium shells, so called due to their similarity to teeth, although they were actually the shell of a marine mollusc, dentalidae or 'tusk shell'.

Dentalium shells, obtained from the Pacific coastal region, were also available through Indian traders at mercantile stores and trading posts. Being conveniently hollow, the dentalia were strung in curved parallel rows over the entire yoke section of the dress, creating a cape-like effect. In some cases, they were used in conjunction with other trade materials such as metal sequins, imported from France. This style of dress was also popular among the Cheyennes. Navy blue trade cloth, for this style, was considered de rigueur.

The sleeves and lower hemline were decorated with bands of colored silk ribbons, sequins, and military style metallic fringe, invariably emphasizing the white selvedge of the cloth. Additionally, further dentalium shells were applied, often forming cross and circle designs to the sleeves and hemline.

A specifically Northern Plains variant of trade cloth dress was a more lightweight dress of cotton sateen. Constructionally, this dress represents a distinct departure from traditional types, no doubt influenced by white American fashions of the period. Indeed, for everyday wear, Blackfeet women wore plain cotton cloth dresses of a similar cut.

The style is characterized by ¾-length closed sleeves and a separately added full skirt with a gathered waist. The yoke was typically applied with parallel lane-stitch lanes of a distinctive type of bead called 'basket beads' (sometimes referred to as 'cane beads' or Sprengperlen).1 Below this were fringes of basket beads, terminating in brass bells or metal thimbles, which were pleasing to the ear when the dress was being worn.

Basket beads were manufactured in Bohemia by the Gablonz glass industries. Measuring between four and six millimeters in diameter, they are hexagonally faceted, the ends somewhat rough and uneven. Interestingly, there are two distinct manufacturing techniques employed to create the different colors. The first type is made of actual colored glass, usually translucent, including light blue, dark blue, various greens, browns, gray, amber, black and white. The second type is made of a transparent colorless glass, with a color applied to the

[1] The word Sprengperlen derives from the German verb absprengen, meaning 'broken off'. The terms 'basket bead' and 'cane bead', however, are preferred when used in the context of Native American material culture. These beads were the subject of an article by Carole Morris and in the BSGB newsletter [Morris 2002].

inside. The manufacturing process for both types involved the glass being drawn out into long canes. For the second type, a colored wash was sucked up inside the glass tube, lending the eventual bead its color. This latter technique produced basket beads of red, pink, pale yellow, orange, and a variety of blues and greens. The canes were then cut down into short lengths.

The same beads were used by a variety of other North American groups during the same period. The Chippewa from the Great Lakes region used them for fringes on bandoleer bags. The Iroquois incorporated them into the beadwork and loop fringe suspensions on pincushions and other 'whimsies' made for sale for the tourist market [Green 2001]; and Plateau groups, as well as several Canadian Plains tribes, used them for fringes on dresses and horse martingales.

For a relatively brief period, perhaps one or two decades in total, from the mid-1890s onwards, basket beads seem to have been one of the favorite materials for the adornment of lightweight cloth dresses. They were sometimes used in conjunction with other decorative devices such as elk teeth, cowrie shells or 'real beads', which produced a particularly pleasing effect. Bugle beads, longer lengths of the same glass canes, were also used to decorate Blackfeet trade cloth dress yokes, sometimes combined with basket beads.

Numerous turn-of-the-century photographs of Blackfeet women wearing sateen dresses at dances and other celebrations bear testimony to their enormous popularity on the Browning Blackfeet reservation.

The basket beads are usually applied in parallel bands of contrasting colors. Decoration often follows the traditional 'deertail' outline, similar to yokes of skin dresses, echoing the downward dip of the animal's tail. Earlier 2-skin (binary) dresses were constructed by sewing two entire hides together, the shoulders being formed by the hind legs of the animal, any

Diagram showing the pattern for a typical Plains woolen trade cloth dress. Constructed from a single length of cloth, it has separately added sleeves and tapered gussets to the sides of the skirt.

surplus skin being folded down, creating an undulating outline, with the tail hanging down at the center. Other examples have a similar outline but with either straight parallel bands or bands forming an arc, rather like a rounded cape.

Below the decorated field are generally suspended buckskin fringes threaded with basket beads and brass bells. Metal thimbles were commonly used instead of brass bells, and produced a similarly pleasing sound and an overall effect of graceful motion.

Horizontal bands of silk ribbon in contrasting colors are often applied to the lower edge of the skirt. This was a common form of treatment of the skirt section of woolen trade cloth and lightweight sateen dresses. Brightly

colored rick-rack braid, and commercial lace were also commonly employed.

A common variant of the Northern trade cloth dress was the separate cape, fully beaded with basket beads in similar fashion to the yoke section of the cloth dress, though often abandoning the deertail outline. Some capes were probably modified from original cloth dresses which had become detached from the skirt after much wear and tear. They were generally worn over a plain cotton dress.

The eventual decline in the use of basket beads, somewhere around 1930, was probably due more to a lack of availability than a conscious choice on the part of the Blackfeet to stop using them. Alternative forms of adornment for Plains trade cloth dresses include French brass trade beads, applied in bands, as well as Indian head cent coins or traders' metal tokens, applied in curved rows.

In the case of the Sioux and Cheyenne, trade cloth dresses were worn in conjunction with broad belts of domed nickel silver conchos, heavy breastplates of vertically-strung bone hairpipes, beaded leggings and moccasins. Northern groups wore them in conjunction with brass tack-decorated or beaded panel belts, beaded leggings and moccasins.

Trade cloth dresses were, for many decades, the ultimate fashion statement among Plains Indian women and, in their blending of Indian and non-Indian materials and influences, created a new and very beautiful style of clothing.

Today, cowrie and dentalium shells, carved bone, molded composition and plastic imitation elk teeth, can be purchased from trading posts and Indian craft suppliers throughout the United States. Cane beads, however, have not been manufactured for many decades. The popularity of the woolen trade cloth dress is as great today as it ever was.

Above: Detail of a piece of 'saved list' trade cloth, made in the woolen mills of northern England, and traded widely to Indians throughout much of North America. Note the undyed white selvedge with saw-tooth effect, resulting from the production process. This selvedge was usually trimmed off when used for European purposes, but was considered highly attractive by Indians, to the extent that they would refuse supplies of cloth if it was not of the desired type.

Detail of elk teeth (or 'tushes') on the Sioux trade cloth dress belonging to Rosy White Thunder. Each elk tooth is pierced with either one or two holes and threaded on thin buckskin lacing or thick commercial cotton thread, used double.

Rosa (or Rosy) White Thunder, Sioux, wearing dress of 'saved list' trade cloth, probably navy blue in color. The yoke section is heavily decorated with elk tushes. Many examples of this style of dress employ a mixture of real and carved imitations. Note the undyed selvedge to the sleeves, as well as the dentalium shell earrings, with thick harness leather spacers, a style in vogue throughout much of the nineteenth century. Also, the multi-strand necklace of French brass trade beads; simple necklace of large glass trade beads; and the broad panel belt of heavy-duty harness leather, decorated with domed brass tacks. Photograph by John Choate, November 1883.

This photograph was taken on the occasion of the young woman's arrival at the notorious Carlisle Indian School in Pennsylvania in November 1883. The photographer, John Choate, took another photograph of Rosa White Thunder a few months later, minus her beautiful Lakota trade cloth dress and accessories. In the later photograph, she wears Euro-American dress. The intention of the two photographs, of course, was to demonstrate the so-called 'civilizing' effect of three months' education at Indian schools such as Carlisle. Ironically, the dress was purchased from Rosa White Thunder by the Carlisle school superintendent, Captain R.H. Pratt, for the sum of forty dollars. It seems the clothing of the Sioux had some intrinsic value after all! The dress is now in the collections of the Smithsonian Institution, Washington D.C. Today, far from being regarded as an 'uncivilized' form of clothing, the trade cloth dress is the choice of many women traditional dancers at modern-day pow wows and, with justification, signifies a profound pride in Native American cultural heritage.

Two Central Plains girls, circa 1890-1910. Both women wear dresses of 'saved list' trade cloth, probably navy blue in color. The yoke of the dress worn by the girl on the left is applied with rows of cowrie shells in much the same fashion as elk tushes. The girl on the right wears a dress with dentalium shell-decorated yoke, the undyed selvedge embellished with ribbonwork and sequins. Both girls also wear bone hairpipe necklaces with harness leather spacers.

Written Heritage Collection.

Late nineteenth century Sioux trade cloth dress with cowrie shell-decorated yoke with added sleeve pieces and gussets to give fulness to the skirt. The extensions of the gussets derive from the untrimmed forelegs used as decorative pendants in the leather form of this style.

Denver Art Museum; BS-152

Detail of cowrie shells applied to the yoke of Teton Sioux woman's dress. Each shell is pierced with a single hole and sewn in place with either a heavy duty commercial thread, used double, or fine buckskin lace.

Denver Art Museum; BS-152

Detail of dentalium shells decorating the yoke section of a Sioux woman's trade cloth dress. Each dentalium, hollow throughout its length, is threaded on thick cotton thread, used double, and applied in compact rows to the woolen trade cloth dress yoke.

Mrs. Left Hand and child, part of a group of Arapahos photographed by Charles Carpenter at the St. Louis Exposition in 1904. Each wears a dentalium shell-decorated dress of navy woolen stroud cloth, the shells arranged in curved parallel rows, threaded on thick cotton thread. Both dresses have ribbon pendants attached to the yoke area, a typical form of embellishment on this style of trade cloth dress. Mrs. Left Hand wears a short necklace of bone hairpipes with brass bead suspensions and metal-framed mirror trim. Both mother and daughter wear nickel silver domed concho belts with long drop, as well as beaded accessories.

Written Heritage Collection

Diagram of a typical Blackfeet sateen dress.

Illustration by Darlene Heriard

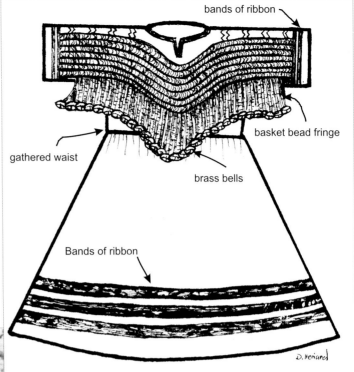

bands of ribbon

basket bead fringe

gathered waist

brass bells

Bands of ribbon

D. Heriard

Blackfeet group, circa 1910. All three women are wearing cloth dresses, the yokes decorated with lanes of basket beads in exaggerated deertail outline. Note the heavy basket bead fringe with suspensions of brass thimbles, as well as the ribbon trim to the hemlines. Photographed by Thomas McGee.
    Written Heritage Collection

In Paint and Feathers
On Tour with Pahaska

The recent hundredth anniversary of a most remarkable historical event passed by almost unnoticed in the important industrial city of Birmingham, at the heart of the English Midlands. For on the last day of May in the year 1903, 'Buffalo Bill' Cody and his Congress of Rough Riders arrived in town. In addition to Mexican vaqueros, cowboys, Bedouins and Cossacks, the extraordinary troupe of performers included large numbers of Sioux Indians, recruited from reservations in South Dakota. A show ground and tipi camp were set up in Perry Barr, on the outskirts of the city, and stayed for two weeks, during which time 'Wild West' performances were given twice daily.

Already acclaimed throughout the United States, Cody had visited Birmingham on two previous occasions, in 1887 and 1891. Both previous tours had also comprised a substantial Sioux presence. The 1903 visit to Birmingham formed part of a European tour that began in December of 1902 and ended in 1905, taking in every town or city of any size throughout Britain.

Newspaper advertisements of the day announced details of the promised spectacle, which boasted of Colonel W. F. Cody's 'New and Interesting Arrangement of the Well-Known Wild West Incidents, Introducing the Pioneers of the Plains, who tell the Story of Progress in the Great Drama of Civilization'.

In this great story, of course, the Sioux, together with other Plains peoples, had been dispossessed of their lands and were embarking reluctantly on a painful process of transition from their former nomadic ways to an enforced sedentary lifestyle on government reservations. Finally crushed after the massacre of nearly two hundred men, women and children by 7th US cavalry forces at Wounded Knee in December 1890, they now faced an uncertain future.

In accordance with their warrior tradition, numbers of Sioux from Pine Ridge and Rosebud agencies in South Dakota sought adventures in faraway lands and an escape from the poverty and squalor of reservation life. Colonel Cody was known to the Sioux as *Pehin' Han'ska,* (contracted to *Pahaska*) or 'Long Hair'. He offered them a season's paid employment in return for their participation in re-enactments of historic battles and wagon train attacks.

One local newspaper, the *Birmingham Pictorial and Dart,* on 12 June 1903, commented on the impact of the Sioux visit to the city:

> *After all is said, there is something remarkable and picturesque about the painted and befeathered heathens which cannot fail to arouse our curiosity. [...] As an object lesson Buffalo Bill's Wild West is undoubtedly valuable, and modern methods of illustration will be able to hand down to posterity true pictures of scenes from Indian life which are rapidly passing away and shortly to become an extinct feature like the buffalo, which has already disappeared from the western Plains.*

Cody's Sioux were attractions wherever they went. Their prominent role in Cody's outfit and their feather-bedecked finery in many ways invented, or at least reinforced, the popular stereotype of the Plains warrior in the European consciousness.

The huge troupe arrived at Witton railway station on 31 May 1903, and set up a 10-acre show ground and encampment in Aston Lane, Perry Barr. The *Birmingham Daily Mail* reported on the event as follows:

THE "WILD WEST" IN BIRMINGHAM - ARRIVAL AT PERRY BARR

The establishment constituting Buffalo Bill's Wild West Show arrived in Birmingham yesterday, and encamped upon the show ground, some ten acres in extent, in Aston Lane, Perry Barr, where it will remain for the next fortnight. No fewer than 800 persons tour with the show, and their conveyance from one place to another and their installation upon new ground is a wonderful example of efficient organisation. On Saturday, "The Wild West" gave two performances at Shrewsbury, at the close of which men, animals and paraphernalia were transferred to Witton. Immediately on arrival the scores of wagons, many of which serve as sleeping quarters, were conveyed to Aston Lane by a magnificent stud of horses, and within a few hours the some two dozen or more large tents which enclose the exhibition ground were pitched, and all necessary arrangements made in the way of seating accommodation. What most impressed the spectators was the smoothness and rapidity with which the work was carried out. Every man knew his task, and did it, and the site having been previously carefully planned, there was not the slightest delay. The site, which is made up of several fields of fine turf land, is a most convenient one. It may be reached by tram or train either to Perry Barr or Witton. The arena is of the most perfect character, being almost as level as a cricket ground, and is 414 feet long, with a width of 180 feet. The arena is entirely in the open air, and two performances will be given daily irrespective of the weather. All the seats are under cover, and occupy a canvas space 500 feet long by 325 feet wide. The last visit to Birmingham of Colonel W.F. Cody was in 1891, when the show was pitched at the Aston Lower Grounds. The present exhibition is indefinitely larger than on first occasion, and possesses many new features. The congress of rough riders comes from all parts of the world. In a walk round the show ground one encounters men representative of almost every nationality and language. The American Indians, decorated with paint and feathers, occupy an encampment to themselves. Their quaint-looking wigwams [sic], bearing all sorts of rudely-drawn pictures, excited much interest.

The first performances took place the following day, and continued twice daily for two weeks. On 2 June, the *Birmingham Daily Mail*

Sioux tipi in the Indian encampment in Aston Lane, Perry Barr, Birmingham, photographed by Alfred Juggins, June 1903. Public Records Office, London

Chief Luther Standing Bear heads the procession of Sioux Indians. His clothing and accessories are typical of those worn by many of Cody's Wild West show Indians. His warbonnet is made of immature golden eagle tail feathers. He wears a cotton shirt and vest, woolen trade cloth leggings with beaded strips, and carries a lightweight muslin shield with eagle tail feather trim. Over the front of the saddle is draped a woolen trade cloth blanket with broad beaded blanket strip, trimmed with lengths of colored silk ribbon.

Photographed by Joseph Thomas Carter, Buffalo Bill Parade, Birmingham, 1903. Courtesy of Birmingham Library Services.

reported on the first performance, held on the previous afternoon:

BUFFALO BILL'S "WILD WEST"

The big "Wild West" show at Perry Barr opened auspiciously, from 10,000 to 11,000 witnessing yesterday's matinée. So great was the throng in the approaches to the show ground that it was difficult to believe any holiday folk could be left in Birmingham. Yet the arrangements for their accommodation were perfect, and the consummate ease and order with which the visitors were seated and finally disposed of was not the least of Buffalo Bill's triumphs. The "rough riders" appeal to popular taste in a quite irresistible way. For two spirit-stirring hours the spectator is kept in a pleasant fever of excitement. He sympathetically "goes the pace" with break-neck riders who scorn danger in their realistic reproduction of the wild delights of the prairie. Moreover, these dare-devil exploits stir within him the latent element of the primeval savage which finds a kind of makeshift satisfaction in the gory delights of *melodrama, or which runs amuk in a racing motor. As a counteraction of humdrum routine the "Wild West" leaves nothing to be desired. It has, moreover, the great merit that it seeks to reproduce that mighty and heroic wrestle with nature which invariably precedes the setting up of our complex civilization. The most fascinating entertainment all the world over is that which reproduces as closely as possible undiluted and unpolished nature, and the best compliment that can be paid the "Wild West" exhibition is that, in addition to being an entertainment, it is a most engrossing and bewitching study. For the first time in his life the spectator yesterday saw enacted scenes, the vivid recital of which by popular historians and novelists had often curtailed his*

Sioux warriors, wearing eagle feather warbonnets and carrying feathered lances, parade past H. Greaves' shop, as amazed Birmingham locals look on. The rider in the foreground also wears a fully-beaded vest, brass cuffs, woolen trade cloth leggings with cut trim and beaded strips, and has a trade cloth blanket with broad beaded blanket strip wrapped around his waist.

Photographed by Joseph Thomas Carter, Buffalo Bill Parade, Birmingham, 1903. Courtesy of Birmingham Library Services.

hours of sleep. So enthralled was he that he almost forgot to applaud. Thousands of pairs of eyes tried to take in that wonderful review of Indian pageantry with which the show opens. The grand review of rough riders—Indians, British Cavalry, Mexicans, Cowboys, Cossacks, and the rest—is immensely imposing, but the Indians above all engross attention. The performers seem themselves to revel in the wild excitement, though compared with the real life and death tussels of the prairie, the racing and sham-fighting must be a very mild tonic. Yet their eyes sparkle, and their rows of pearly teeth gleam with unmistakable pleasure. The massive and stalwart build and athletic bearing of these redskins make a great impression on the spectator, suggesting afresh the query how so physically perfect a race could tend toward extinction as they are so obviously doing. Another question which suggested itself to many who heard their half-terrible, half-grotesque war whoop for the first time is by what queer anomaly and paradox such burly fellows should come to have such high-pitched voices.

On 8 June, large crowds gathered to witness a spectacular parade through the city's main streets.

The procession left Aston Lane by way of Birchfield Road and passed down Alma Street, Summer Lane, up Snow Hill, along Colmore Row, down New Street, into Corporation Street, Aston Street, Aston Road, Park Road, Witton Lane, finally returning to Aston Lane in time for the afternoon performance.

A local photographer named Joseph Thomas Carter recorded the procession for posterity, positioned with his hand-held camera in New Street, opposite Henry Greaves' portmanteaux premises, near the corner of Corporation Street. Judging by the expressions of awe on their faces, the occasion was an experience never to be forgotten in the lives of the assembled crowd of 'Brummies'.

At the forefront of the parade was Colonel Cody, in an American barouche carriage drawn by two white horses, followed by the Indians, led by the famous Oglala Sioux chief, actor and advocate, Luther Standing Bear. Charged by Cody to keep good order among the Sioux members of the troupe, Standing Bear is well

known for his success in making the transition between the world of the Indian and that of the white man, without losing touch with his Sioux heritage. Both he and his wife, Laura, appear in 'Buffalo Bill's Wild West' postcards, published to publicize the tours. (See photos on page 44, 45,46,and 47).

In his book, *My People the Sioux*, first published in 1928, Standing Bear relates the following moving story of his two-week stay in Birmingham:

After a time the show reached Birmingham. This was a beautiful city, but we had an arena there. While we were showing in Birmingham, a little daughter was born to us. The morning papers discussed the event in big headlines that the first full-blooded Indian baby had been born at the Buffalo Bill show grounds. Colonel Cody was to be its godfather and the baby was to be named after the reigning Queen of England. The child's full name was to be Alexandra Birmingham Cody Standing Bear.

The next morning Colonel Cody came to me and asked if my wife and baby could be placed in the side-show. He said the English people would like to see the face of a newly born Indian baby lying in an Indian cradle or 'hoksicala postan'. I gave my consent, and the afternoon papers stated that the baby and mother could be seen the following afternoon.

Long before it was time for the show to begin, people were lining up in the road. My wife sat on a raised platform, with the little one in the cradle before her. The people filed past, many of them dropping money in a box for her. Nearly every one had some sort of little gift for her also. It was a great drawing card for the show; the work was very light for my wife, and as for the baby, before she was twenty-four hours old she was making more money than my wife and I together.

With the coming of the new baby came added cares, of course. Our little boy, who was named after me (Luther), had to be rigged up for the part he took in the show. He had a full costume of buckskin, very much like the one I wore, and every day his face must be painted and his hair combed and braided for the two performances. The Indian boys seemed to think it was a pleasure to get the little chap ready for exhibition. After he was 'all fixed up', he would stand outside the tipi, and the English people would crowd around to shake his hand and give him money. This he would put in a little pocket in his buckskin jacket, and when it was full he would refuse to accept any more, although the crowd would try to force it on him. Then he would leave, in apparent disgust, and come inside the tipi. He kept us all laughing.

Buffalo Bill's 'Wild West' continued its twice daily performances until 13 June, when the entire outfit was dismantled, the troupe returned to Witton railway station to rejoin the train to Worcester, where the show was to open on 15 June.

The warbonnet-wearing figure in the foreground of this photograph wears a bone hairpipe breastplate, woolen trade cloth leggings with beaded strips, and fully-beaded moccasins. He carries a feather-trimmed staff and muslin shield decorated with trade cloth and eagle feathers. Behind him, the rider on the extreme left wears a fully-beaded vest. The central figure wears a bone hairpipe breastplate and a muslin shield slung over his back. The other rider, holding a long fur-wrapped lance, wears a breastplate of otter fur, decorated with metal-framed mirrors. Across their chests, the horses wear martingales trimmed with large metal bells.
Photographed by Joseph Thomas Carter, Buffalo Bill Parade, Birmingham, 1903. Courtesy of Birmingham Library Services.

Some Honor I Seek
Sioux Indians in Early Postcards

One of the major contributing factors in the dissemination of information concerning North American Indians in the closing years of the nineteenth century was a popular novelty in the form of the picture postcard. Huge numbers of these postcards, usually bearing lithographically produced images of Indian subjects, were produced in the United States, Canada and Europe over a prolonged period, the heyday being the period between 1900 and 1920.

In our modern age of mass-media and electronic communication, it is perhaps difficult to comprehend fully the role of the postcard in early twentieth century social life, when the visual impact of mass-produced photographic images was beginning to be appreciated for the first time. Affordably priced and on sale in every local stationer's store, picture postcards were available to all and, prior to widespread use of the telephone, served as a popular and effective means of communication between family and friends. For the price of a postage stamp, (one cent for destinations within the United States, Canada and Mexico), cards posted to local addresses in the morning were generally delivered later in the same day. For an additional cent, postcards could be sent to loved ones in foreign countries, relating news of the sender's fortunes and experiences.

With their exotic and colorful themes, postcards were avidly collected. North American Indians, particularly Plains Indians, were popular subjects. The prominence of the Sioux in traveling shows such as W.F. Cody's 'Wild West', as well as countless state fairs and international exhibitions, fostered a general stereotype of this particular nation as the archetypal 'Plains Indian'. Images of Indians dressed in southern Teton Sioux-style regalia, including eagle feather warbonnets, beaded vests, broadcloth leggings and blankets, led to the widespread misconception that *all* Native Americans wore this style of clothing.

From a random sample of postcard images with an American Indian theme, a large percentage has Teton Sioux Indians, or Indians dressed in Teton Sioux-style regalia, as their subject. By far the most recurrent subjects are 'chiefs' and 'warriors'. Although this male emphasis was overriding, other favorite subjects include portraits of Indian women and children, as well as scenes of Indian dances.

As might be expected, the quality of these images varies. Some cards, although based on actual photographic portraits, were gaudily over-painted with unrealistic colors, presumably to enhance the exotic appeal of the finished product. Incongruously, a few examples were even embellished with the addition of glitter. These forms of decoration, however, are intrusive and detract from the reliability of the visual information contained in the image.

Moreover, the identification of the subjects of many early portrait postcards is often quite inaccurate. In certain cases, details of the specific tribal origin of individual Indian subjects are incorrectly recorded, the reliability of this sort of information often being a secondary consideration, as long as the caption on the card proclaimed an exotic-sounding Indian name!

The British firm of Raphael Tuck and Sons Ltd, based in Moorfields, London, published several different series of warbonnet-wearing chiefs. Marketed as 'Oilettes', these chromo-lithographic postcards were artist-drawn re-workings of original photographic portraits. As well as their offices in London and Paris, Tuck's also established offices in New York in 1900, and used American artists to design many of their cards, although the majority were printed in England, Germany and Saxony. Their 'Indian Chiefs' series included, among others, fine quality portraits of the Sioux leaders, Hollow Horn, Iron Owl and Black Thunder.

Tuck's 'Hiawatha' series, featuring captions drawn from Longfellow's epic poem based on Indian legend from the Great Lakes region, strangely confuses the issue by illustrating alongside each quotation a Plains Indian 'chief' wearing eagle feather warbonnet. The unidentified Sioux individuals who feature in this series are possibly William F Cody's seasonal 'Wild West' show recruits. This somewhat misinformed blurring of cultural references is an all-too-common phenomenon, and has contributed to the perpetual misrepresentation of Native Americans.

Large numbers of souvenir postcards were produced to advertise Buffalo Bill's 'Wild West' tours of the United States, Canada and Europe. Cody's flair for publicity was impressive, in common with his other logistical skills that made his touring show such a success. A series of monochrome cards was published to coincide with the 1902-03 season British tour, available in stationers' stores throughout the country long in advance of the troupe's arrival. The series comprises full-length portraits of Luther Standing Bear, Lone Bear, Black Bird, Sands Rock, and two separate images of Luther's wife, Laura, the second with the couple's young son, Luther Standing Bear Junior.

The aforementioned series of cards have undivided backs; a year later, for the 1904 season tour, the same series had divided backs.

Many of the Sioux members of Cody's troupe, although not actually chiefs, were nevertheless described as such in the captions to the postcards. This was the case in much of the other publicity material relating to the shows, and Indians were routinely promoted as 'chiefs' and even as members of other tribal groups, even though only Sioux Indians accompanied Cody to Britain and Europe.

In 1904, Weiner's Ltd, of Acton, London, published a series of colored cards to promote the tour of Great Britain. Versions of the same cards were also produced in other European languages to promote the ensuing European tour. These cards were copyrighted by Barnum & Bailey Ltd, with whom Cody's outfit had collaborated by this time. The set consists of six artist-drawn cards of Indian subjects, plus another card of Cody on horseback, all contained in a souvenir envelope. The Indian cards, all untitled and rather fancifully contrived, include a full-length portrait of Luther Standing Bear, holding lance and feather-trimmed shield; another of Laura Standing Bear, seated with child in a cradle; a head-and-shoulders portrait of an unidentified Sioux man, holding a tomahawk; a head-and-shoulders profile of the Sioux chief, Red Shirt, who toured with Cody in previous years; a rather naïve image of a warbonnet-wearing warrior on horseback; and a scene of Indians attacking the Deadwood stagecoach. Interestingly, several of the Indians in these images seem to be wearing numbered identity medals.

Numerous postcards were produced depicting the Oglala Sioux chief, Iron Tail or *Sinte Maza*, some dating from his later years with 101 Ranch, when he was lauded as 'The Indian on the Buffalo Nickel'. Another image, probably published in the 1920s, shows Iron Tail standing talking to Cody, seated in his tent.

The German publisher, W. Schinkmann, issued an interesting series of color postcards of the pre-show parades through the streets of European towns in which Cody's Indians and the 'Wild West' spectacle performed. Iron Tail is pictured at the head of the procession in one of these cards. Each card bears a caption in German.

A host of American publishers issued their own series of American Indian cards. One interesting set of colored cards was issued between 1903-05, based on images copyrighted by the photographer, F.A. Rinehart of Omaha, Nebraska. Sensitively over-painted, subjects include Big Man, Bill Rock, Chase-in-the-Morning, Sitting Bull, Clear, Rain-in-the-Face, Yellow Wolf, Annie Red Shirt, a small girl named Lost Bird, another image of Lost Bird with her mother, and the Apache chief, Geronimo.

Another very fine series was produced by E.J. Freiburg of Chicago in 1901, copyrighted by John F. Byrnes & Co. The subjects include

Iron Tail, Black Fox, Mr and Mrs Little Red Cloud, and Kills Enemy, (the latter's tribal affiliation wrongly identified as Blood rather than Sioux).

The postcards illustrated here bear testimony to the large number of publishers from all over the United States, Canada and Europe, all producing printed material with a Plains Indian theme. In spite of flaws resulting from their status as mass-produced souvenirs, they remain an important visual source of information about Plains Indians at a time of great cultural change.

Chief Black Thunder, wearing eagle feather warbonnet, bone hairpipe breastplate, and holding pipe and tobacco bag. Published by Raphael Tuck and Sons Ltd, 'Indian Chiefs' series.

Chief Hollow Horn, wearing widely flaring warbonnet, fringed jacket, silk neck scarf and two peace medals. Published by Raphael Tuck and Sons Ltd, 'Indian Chiefs' series.

Above: Chief Iron Owl, wearing eagle feather warbonnet with beaded browband, silk scarf, and two peace medals. He holds a catlinite pipe. Published by Raphael Tuck and Sons Ltd, 'Indian Chiefs' series.

Above right: This is one of the 'Hiawatha' series of 'Oilette' cards issued by Raphael Tuck and Sons Ltd. The caption reads: *"Never any deed of daring, But Himself had done a bolder."–Song of Hiawatha. – Longfellow.* In spite of this reference to Longfellow's epic poem inspired by Great Lakes legend, the image depicts a Plains Indian wearing feather warbonnet.

Left: Chief Black Bird, with Buffalo Bill's Wild West, from a series of monochrome postcards published for the 1902-03 British tour. He is pictured wearing a beaded hide war shirt and eagle feather warbonnet. He holds, in one hand, a fur-wrapped feathered lance, in the other a pipe and heavily beaded tobacco bag. Around his waist is tied a muslin dance shield, the gathered folds of the reverse of the shield just visible. [1]

[1] This shirt was eventually collected by James Hooper, and is illustrated in the Hooper Collection catalog [Phelps, 1976: plate 212; p.352, no. 1690.]

CHIEF SANDS ROCK.
WITH BUFFALO BILL'S WILD WEST.

CHIEF LONE BEAR.
WITH BUFFALO BILL'S WILD WEST.

CHIEF STANDING BEAR.
WITH BUFFALO BILL'S WILD WEST

Above left: Chief Sands Rock, with Buffalo Bill's Wild West, from a series of monochrome postcards published for the 1902-03 British tour. Sands Rock is dressed in eagle feather warbonnet, woolen cloth blanket with beaded blanket strip, bone hairpipe breastplate, trade cloth leggings and fully-beaded moccasins.

Above: Chief Lone Bear, with Buffalo Bill's Wild West, from a series of monochrome postcards published for the British tour of 1902-03. Lone Bear wears typical southern Teton Sioux regalia favored by Cody's recruits—eagle feather warbonnet, cloth shirt, hairpipe breastplate, silk scarf, woolen blanket and leggings, and fully-beaded moccasins. The lance with feathers mounted on a strip of colored woolen cloth was a commonly used accessory for 'Wild West' performances. Lone Bear was the subject of a fine photographic portrait by Gertrude Käsebier, taken in New York in 1895. [Hathaway, 1990: p.75].

Left: Chief Standing Bear, with Buffalo Bill's Wild West, from a series of monochrome postcards published for the British tour of 1902-03. Luther Standing Bear was a prominent Sioux member of Cody's troupe. He eventually wrote a number of books about Sioux culture [Standing Bear, 1928]. Although referred to as a chief in the caption to this card, he was in actual fact only made a chief in 1905. His clothing, consisting of store-bought cloth shirt, trailer warbonnet of eagle tail feathers, woolen trade cloth leggings with beaded strips, and fully-beaded moccasins, is typical of Sioux regalia from the early twentieth century. He holds an eagle wing fan and a fur-wrapped lance, probably the same lance carried by Sands Rock on the previous card.

LAURA STANDING BEAR.
With BUFFALO BILL'S WILD WEST.

Laura Standing Bear and Standing Bear, Jr.
With BUFFALO BILL'S WILD WEST.

YOUNG EAGLE (Indian Interpreter).

Above: Laura Standing Bear, with Buffalo Bill's Wild West, from a series of monochrome postcards published for the British tour of 1902-03. Laura was the wife of Luther Standing Bear, and accompanied him on the 1902-03 leg of the British tour. She wears a woolen trade cloth dress, the yoke heavily decorated with dentalium shells. Around her waist is a floral-patterned shawl.

Above right: Laura Standing Bear and Standing Bear, Jr., with Buffalo Bill's Wild West. From a series of monochrome postcards published for the British tour of 1902-03. Laura's young son, Luther Jr., wears a bone breastplate, cloth vest, woolen trade cloth leggings and beaded moccasins—exact child-sized versions of Sioux adult regalia.

Right: Young Eagle, Indian interpreter. This unmarked monochrome card was probably produced in Britain around the time of Cody's 1902-04 visits to Britain, and seems to have been issued by the publishers of the above series, although it bears no reference to Buffalo Bill's 'Wild West'. Young Eagle is dressed in Sioux style regalia, including warbonnet, otter breastplate with metal-framed trade mirrors, cloth shirt, beaded cuffs, woolen trade cloth leggings, part-beaded moccasins. Under his arm he carries a woolen trade cloth blanket; in his left hand a dance wand.

Above right: This artist-drawn postcard belongs to a set of colored cards issued by Weiner's Ltd for the 1904 season tour of Britain and copyrighted by Barnum & Bailey Ltd. The images were presumably based on actual studio photographs. The Sioux individual is unidentified except for a medal bearing the number '329'. He wears a bear claw necklace, cloth shirt, bone hairpipe breastplate and metal cuffs and armbands. In his hair are two eagle tail feathers. He holds a tomahawk with decorative wrapping to the shaft.

Above: This card, also from the Weiner's series, shows the Sioux chief, Red Shirt, not present during the 1902-04 British tour, although he toured with Cody on previous visits. He is impressively dressed in eagle warbonnet and beaded hide war shirt, and wears a peace medal around his neck. He also wears two metal badges, pinned to his shirt, one inscribed 'Chief 25'.

Left: This card from the 1904 Weiner's series shows Luther Standing Bear, standing against a silhouetted background of tipis. He wears a trailer warbonnet, cloth shirt, trade cloth leggings, and moccasins, and holds a lance in one hand, a feather-decorated shield at his waist. The image seems to have been based on the monochrome image of Standing Bear on page 44, although the details of clothing and colors are inaccurately represented. For example, the moccasins he wears in this image are of a Woodland type, not Sioux. This detail was doubtless overlooked by the artist.

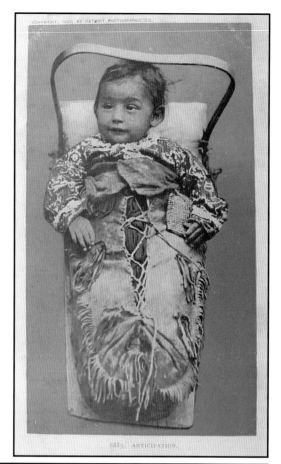

Above: Laura Standing Bear was the wife of Luther Standing Bear. This card was published in 1904 as part of the Weiner's series, after the great interest shown in the birth of her baby in Perry Barr, Birmingham in 1903. The image is based on the monochrome postcards of Mrs. Standing Bear shown on page 45. Her moccasins are inaccurately drawn, and the cradle and baby are copied from a separate postcard illustrating an Ojibwa baby. Sioux cradles, of course, are quite different in appearance. This confusion of tribally specific detail on the part of the artist is a common occurrence.

Above right: Postcard of an Ojibwa baby in its wooden cradle. This image, published by the Detroit Photographic Co. in 1903, provided the detail for the previous postcard of Laura Standing Bear with her baby, the artist obviously assuming that all North American cradles looked the same!

Right: This striking monochrome postcard shows the Oglala Sioux chief, Iron Tail, a close friend of William Cody's and a popular subject for picture postcards in the early years of the twentieth century. He accompanied the 'Wild West' showman on the 1904 leg of the British tour. The handsome chief is wearing a plain cotton shirt, bone hairpipe breastplate, silk scarf and narrow quilled armbands. He wears his hair in characteristic style, braided and tied up. Publisher unknown.

IRON TAIL.
THE FAMOUS INDIAN CHIEF.

Another portrait postcard of Iron Tail, published in 1955 by Stillwater Engraving Company, Oklahoma, from an original negative in 1914 while the Sioux chief was involved with the 101 Ranch. He wears a fringed buckskin shirt, and an eagle tail feather in his hair.

This card of Iron Tail was published by the Illustrated Postal Card Co., New York, and was probably printed in Germany. He is pictured holding a lance decorated with eagle feathers, and wears a warbonnet, bone breastplate, plain cloth shirt, silk scarf, with a beaded trade cloth blanket around his waist.

CHIEF IRON TAIL, INDIAN SQUAWS AND PAPOOSES
AT BUFFALO BILL'S WILD WEST

Above: This well-known postcard shows Iron Tail with a group of Sioux women and children, with the 'Wild West' tented arena in the background. Four of the women are dressed in dentalium shell decorated woolen trade cloth dresses with patterned shawls, typical of Sioux women's clothing of the period. Although the publisher is unidentified, this card was almost certainly on sale at Cody's 'Wild West' performances in the United States in the first decade of the twentieth century.

Chief Iron Tail, Wife and Boy, and the 101 Ranch Bison.

Left: This real photo postcard shows Iron Tail with his wife and son at the 101 Ranch. After the issue of the 'buffalo nickel' in 1913, for which Iron Tail was one of the Indian models, the chief was often associated with the 101 Ranch bison, and cited as 'the Indian on the buffalo nickel'. Iron Tail wears a trailer warbonnet, plain store-bought cloth vest, and trade cloth leggings with beaded strips. His son wears a fully-beaded vest, store-bought cotton shirt and woolen cloth leggings, and his wife a trade cloth dress with elk tush decoration. A bone hairpipe breastplate is worn around her neck. Possibly published by Kraus Manufacturing Co.

83377

Above: This postcard showing Iron Tail with Colonel Cody was published by Curteich-Chicago, copyrighted by Johnny Baker, Golden, Colorado, some years after the death of both Cody and Iron Tail. Iron Tail is dressed in trailer warbonnet, cloth shirt, bone hairpipe breastplate, woolen trade cloth leggings and full-beaded moccasins. Cody is pictured, seated in the opening of his tent, dressed in typical floral-beaded jacket and riding boots.

Right: Chief Iron Tail, photographed by E.J. Freiburg of Chicago, copyrighted by John F. Byrne & Co. in 1901, and printed in Germany. The photograph is one of a series probably taken in Freiburg's studio during 'Wild West' tour in the Chicago area. Iron Tail is pictured, in characteristic dress, comprising eagle bonnet, bone breastplate, striped cotton shirt, and woolen blanket with beaded blanket strip. He also holds a beaded tobacco bag in one hand, a feathered lance in the other.

Iron Tail, on the right, with Black Fox, photographed by E.J. Freiburg, Chicago, and copyrighted by John F. Byrne & Co. in 1901. Both chiefs wear similar Sioux regalia and carry feather staffs.

Left: Kills Enemy, photographed by E.J. Freiburg, Chicago, and copyrighted by John F. Byrne & Co. in 1901. Despite the caption identifying him as a Blood, Kills Enemy was a Sioux. He wears a hair roach and unusual necklace of porcupine guard hair, his body painted, and a muslin shield slung over his shoulder. Several old photographs illustrate muslin dance shields being worn in this manner.

Below: The couple in this photograph, identified here as Mr. and Mrs. Little Red Cloud, were photographed by E.J. Freiburg of Chicago. The postcard was copyrighted by John F. Byrne & Co. in 1901. Another card in the same series depicts the same man, identified as Luke Little Hawk. Identification of Indian individuals was often suspect. In this image, the man wears an otter breastplate with metal-framed trade mirror and silk ribbon decoration, over a plain store-bought shirt. His wife wears typical Sioux style dentalium shell-decorated woolen cloth dress with a bone hairpipe necklace.

Buffalo Bill's Wild West. Indianer

Above: This is one of a series of cards published by W. Schinkmann in Germany, for the 1905 European tour. It shows a parade of Sioux, led by Iron Tail, wearing long trailer warbonnet and carrying a feather-decorated lance, processing through the streets of a French city or town, probably Paris.

Right: This colored card was published for Buffalo Bill's Wild West, probably in 1905, during the extensive European tour. The inscription is in French. The image is an artist-drawn depiction of a Sioux warrior, wearing cloth vest, woolen trade cloth blanket, and holding a spiral-wrapped lance. The detail of the moccasins and leggings, just visible below the blanket, is incorrectly represented.

S. Dakota Sioux Chief.

No. 896. Nat. Art Views Co. N. Y. City.

Left: This card, although identifying the subject merely as a 'S. Dakota Sioux chief', shows Luther Standing Bear wearing a beautiful trailer warbonnet, wool trade cloth blanket and leggings. It was published by the National Art Views Co., New York, and was printed in Germany, probably circa 1902-07.

650 – SIOUX INDIAN CHIEF "STANDING BEAR".

May 12 08
Los Angeles
California

Right: Another portrait of Luther Standing Bear, published and copyrighted by Edward H. Mitchell of San Francisco, 1907. The card is postally used and dated 12th May 1908. The artist-drawn image appears to be based on the previous photograph.

Group of Sioux Indian Chiefs.

Above: Sioux regalia as widely worn for 'Wild West' performances is exemplified in this image of five Sioux Indians, published by the Illustrated Postal Card Co., New York. Almost certainly 'Wild West' recruits, each warrior wears eagle feather warbonnet, cloth shirt and woolen trade cloth leggings, as well as carrying a muslin dance shield and feathered lance.

Left: Produced by the Illustrated Postal Card Co., New York, this card shows a Sioux individual who is known to have toured with Cody's 'Wild West' troupe. He is seen brandishing a revolver, doubtless at the suggestion of the photographer. The warbonnet, otter breastplate, beaded broadcloth blanket and fully-beaded moccasins are all typical Sioux regalia from the late nineteenth and early twentieth century.

Left: The caption to this card identifies this Sioux man as Takes Enemy, Toka-Wicakin, 'in war paint'. Publisher details are given as William H. Rau, 1901. Takes Enemy is dressed for a dance and wears a hair ornament with eagle plumes, old-style dance bustle, trade cloth leggings and ribbon-decorated breechcloth. He carries a dance staff and muslin dance shield.

Right: These Sioux men, identified as Marshal Rising Hand, Mark Setting Spider and Jim Sweetgrass, toured Britain and Europe with Miller Brothers' 101 Ranch in the first decade of the 20th century. All three men wear beaded hide shirts and eagle feather warbonnets. The printed inscription on the verso states that 'their tribe is dwindling in numbers and it will be but a short time before it is altogether extinct.' Probably published by Miller Brothers' 101 Ranch.

MARSHAL RISING HAND   MARK SETTING SPIDER   JIM SWEETGRASS

This Sioux couple, identified as Mr. and Mrs. Owns Many Horses, were participants in the 'Red Man's Spectacle' at Earls Court in London in 1909. This card was published by Gale & Polden Ltd. The man is dressed in cloth shirt, trade cloth blanket and leggings, and fully-beaded moccasins. In his hair, he wears ostrich feathers, probably at the suggestion of the photographer, and carries a finely beaded and quilled tobacco bag. His wife's trade cloth dress is decorated with elk teeth, and around her neck she wears a bone hairpipe necklace. Her outfit is complemented by a nickel silver concho belt, fully-beaded moccasins and patterned shawl.

Sole Survivors of the Black Hawk Massacre Episode. Now taking part in the Red Man Spectacle-Earls Court.

Above: A group of Sioux participants in the 'Red Man's Spectacle' at Earls Court, London, 1909. Published by Gale & Polden Ltd. The man on the extreme left is Red Shirt, wearing hide shirt, loop necklace and trade cloth leggings. The man next to him wears a fine jacket beaded with mounted horsemen, human figures and horses. The man at far right, Painted Horse, wears a beaded hide shirt and leggings and impressive trailer bonnet made of eagle primary feathers.

Left: This is one of a series of embossed and colored cards of Sioux chiefs, copyrighted in 1906 by Welbon Fowcett. This example shows Hollow Horn Bear. In each case, the image suffers from poor quality coloring. The same trailer warbonnet, bone breastplate and beaded tobacco bag are used in each image in the series, these probably being photographer's props.

HIGH PIPE SIOUX CHIEF

Above: Another card in the Welbon Fowcett embossed series of 1906, this one depicting Tall Mandan. The quality of the applied coloring is particularly unfortunate in this example. The regalia is the same as that worn by Hollow Horn Bear in the previous card.

Above right: This postcard, bearing the image of High Pipe, belongs to a similar 'Chiefs' series published by W.G. MacFarlane of New York, Toronto and Buffalo, using the same images as the Fowcett series. Again, the applied colored detail is poorly executed.

Right: This card of Tall Crane is one of a series published in 1909 by the Adolph Selige Publishing Co., St Louis. The fine portrait is marred somewhat by gaudily applied coloring and the addition of glitter. Tall Crane wears a trailer warbonnet, beaded vest with U.S. flag decoration, patterned cotton cloth shirt and trade cloth leggings. He holds a pipe, tobacco bag and trade cloth blanket.

CHIEF "TALL CRANE."

CHIEF "SKIN COTE."

CIRCLING BEAR.

Copyrighted 1903, F. A. Rinehart, Omaha, Neb.

Above: Another card published by Adolph Selige Publishing Co. of St Louis in 1909. The man, identified as 'Skin Cote', is pictured with the same trailer warbonnet, tobacco bag and pipe as in the previous image of Tall Crane. He also wears an otter fur breastplate with metal-rimmed mirrors, and a striped cotton shirt. Photographers often kept their own collections of props with which to kit out their subjects. As in the case of the previous image, this card also has applied glitter decoration.

Above right: This postcard of Circling Bear was published by E. Frey & Co. of New York, and was postmarked at Niagara Falls, 17th October 1904. Circling Bear is shown wearing a split horn bonnet trimmed with ermine skins, with a long trailer of eagle tail feathers. He also wears moccasins with quilled stripes within a beaded border, and holds a pipe with large catlinite bowl.

Left: One of a large series of cards published from photographs copyrighted by F.A. Rinehart of Omaha, Nebraska. This one, of Big Man, was issued in 1903. The skillfully colored image interprets well the details of Big Man's warbonnet with dyed eagle plumes and ermine pendants, silk scarf, otter breastplate and fully-beaded vest.

Copyrighted 1903, F. A. Rinehart, Omaha, Neb.

Copyrighted 1905, F. A. Rinehart, Omaha, Neb.

Copyrighted 1905, F. A. Rinehart, Omaha, Neb.

Above: Chase-in-the-Morning, with quilled hair ornament, bow case and quiver, and shield. The shield, with buckskin cover decorated with quilled concentric lines and eagle feather trim, is a familiar prop that appears in several of Rinehart's photographs.

Above right: Annie Red Shirt, wearing finely beaded and fringed hide dress and bone hairpipe necklace. Copyrighted by F.A. Rinehart, Omaha, Nebraska, 1905.

Right: Lost Bird, wearing trade cloth dress ornamented with elk teeth, sequins and ribbonwork, beaded leggings and moccasins. Copyrighted by F.A. Rinehart, Omaha, Nebraska, 1905.

"KICKING BEAR."

"NO NECK" CHIEF.

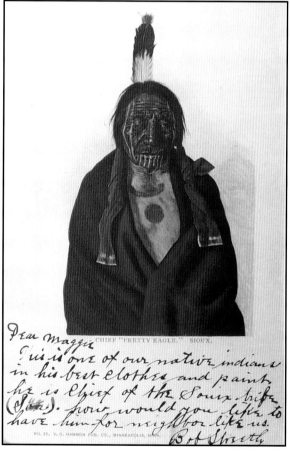

CHIEF "PRETTY EAGLE." SIOUX.

Above left: Kicking Bear, wearing plain cloth shirt, silk neck scarf and bone hairpipe breastplate. The publisher, although unidentified on the card, is probably E.C. Kropp of Milwaukee. The card bears a postmark of 17th October 1907 and an inscription in Danish.

Above right: No Neck, dressed in trailer warbonnet, bone hairpipe breastplate, plain cloth shirt and otter fur chest ornament and holding an ornate pipe with pewter inlay to bowl and stem carved with symbolic elk and turtle motifs. Published by E.C. Kropp of Milwaukee and postmarked 28th July 1901.

Left: Pretty Eagle, with a single eagle feather in his hair, his braids wrapped in woolen trade cloth. The extensive face and body paint may have been added by the artist who retouched the original image on behalf of the publisher. Published by V.O. Hammon Publishing Co. of Minneapolis, Minnesota.

Eagle Boy, Sioux.
S.S. Umbria swept by Mountainous waves, 1 Sailor in
hurt, passing in fright, child died nigger ripped away.

EAGLE TRACK.

Chief Pontiac
1720 - 1769.

Above: This postcard bears a splendidly colored portrait of a man identified as Eagle Boy, wearing a warbonnet, otter fur breastplate with metal-framed trade mirrors, fully-beaded vest with geometric design, silk neckerchief and metal armbands. Published by H.C. Leighton Co., Portland, Maine, printed in Germany, and postmarked 15th December 1905.

Above right: Eagle Track in full Sioux regalia comprising eagle feather warbonnet with quilled browband, bone breastplate, woolen cloth blanket with beaded blanket strip, and holding a beaded tobacco bag and pipe with catlinite bowl and quilled stem. Probably published by Raphael Tuck & Sons Ltd., circa 1903.

Right: This real photo postcard shows Hollow Horn Bear, dressed in warbonnet, bone breastplate and beaded war shirt trimmed with hairlocks and an eagle tail feather. The sender was apparently under the misapprehension that the portrait was of Chief Pontiac. Photographed by F.A. Rinehart, Omaha, Nebraska, 1898.

This monochrome card was published for the Brussels Exhibition of 1935 and depicts Chief White Buffalo Man and his wife, standing in front of a Sioux tipi. The woman is dressed in the finest Sioux regalia—a fully-beaded buckskin dress with heavy bone hairpipe necklace. Her husband wears a double-trailer warbonnet, beaded hide shirt, woolen trade cloth leggings and beaded moccasins. He holds a stone-headed club and mirror-decorated otter fur breastplate. The card is signed 'White Buffalo Man'.

Left: This real photo card shows Luke Arrow, resplendent in eagle feather bonnet trimmed with ermine fur, quilled shirt with added 'white man's' collar, and otter breastplate with metal-framed mirrors. In one hand he holds a fan made from a complete eagle's tail, a wooden pipe stem in the other. Photographed by Miller, Pierre, South Dakota.

Below: This real photo card is one of a number depicting the same group of Indians at Mandan, North Dakota, all photographed by Lutz, probably in the 1930s or 40s. The group seems to be dressed to entertain visitors disembarking from the railway, just visible in the background. If indeed they are Sioux, their clothing reflects influence from neighboring tribes to the north. Three of the men wear loop necklaces. The very long hairpipe necklaces worn by the women were particularly popular for several decades with certain Sioux groups in North Dakota.

Real photo postcard of Sioux Indians dancing at Cheyenne Frontier Days, Wyoming, in 1949. The dancers wear a variety of styles of dance outfit. One man, at left, wears a double trailer warbonnet, rarely seen among the Sioux in more recent years. He also wears a beaded vest with pictographic designs, and matching cuffs. The fourth dancer from the left is dressed in a bonnet, beaded shirt and leggings, and holds a tobacco bag. The remaining dancers wear old-time dance outfits with roaches and bustles, several with dyed long-johns.

Copyrighted by De Vere

White Man's Vision
Evolving Stereotypes of the Plains Indian

I am of another nation. When I speak, you do not understand me. When you speak, I do not understand you. - Spokan Garry, Spokane chief

The whites told only one side. Told it to please themselves. Told much that is not true. Only his best deeds, only the worst deeds of the Indians, has the white man told. - Yellow Wolf, Nez Perce

The Native American has long been an object of fascination for non-Native people, and images of Indians abound in the popular media. They vary greatly in nature, ranging from the romanticized portrait of the 'Noble Savage' to the inherently racist depiction of the 'bloodthirsty barbarian'.

Early representations, idealized by the eighteenth century French philosophers such as Jean-Jacques Rousseau, endowed the Indian with a gentle, childlike innocence, living in complete harmony with nature. This rather benign stereotype of the Indian as early environmentalist and 'steward' of the land would prove to be one of the most enduring. Embodied within it, however, was the basic belief in the cultural supremacy of European civilization.

As European expansion into Native territories accelerated in the nineteenth century—moving inexorably westward—these stereotypes became much less sympathetic. Indians, determined to fight for their lands, stood in the way of the colonization process and were viewed as an impediment to 'progress' and 'civilization'. As such they were routinely represented as 'savages', noble or otherwise.

After the fateful battle of the Little Big Horn in Montana on 25 June 1876, in which George Armstrong Custer and his 7th US Cavalry lost over 250 men to the combined forces of Sioux and Cheyennes, hysterical newspaper reports further east spoke of the slayers of Custer as 'heathens'. The full fury of the humiliated and outraged white world was now unleashed, and a new agenda, that of eradicating the indigenous peoples from the Plains, was set. And with this gathering of military might came a sinister process of denigration that had a very deliberate purpose—that of de-humanizing the indigenous inhabitants of the North American continent.

One late nineteenth century writer [Brown, n.d.: 72] wrote the following description of the Indian character:

The American Indians have usually been described as stolid and impassive, and to a passing stranger they really appear so; but once let the suspicion and reserve wear off, and they are far from reserved in their behavior. When excited, they have no control over themselves, and are mere creatures of impulse, scarcely answerable for their acts. A trifle, which would never affect a white man, would with an Indian act like a spark to a gunpowder magazine. One moment he is stolid, the next excited and wild.

No one was left in any doubt as to the colonizers' intentions—whites were whipped up into a frenzy of hatred and what followed saw the near destruction of a people who had occupied the continent for eons.

Paradoxically, there was an enormous demand among Europeans for images and other curios of Native people. Photographs, in the form of cartes-de-visite and stereoscopic slides, popular from the 1860s, allowed non-Native Americans and Europeans to appreciate, at a safe distance, the fierce splendor of the flamboyant 'barbarians'.

By the late nineteenth century, when the West had been 'tamed' and the indigenous populations finally defeated and confined on government reservations, Indians were perceived as a broken, dispossessed people, members of a rapidly vanishing race with little or no part to play in the modern world. Zealous anthropologists and photographers began to document the cultures of these 'doomed' peoples before they eventually disappeared forever into oblivion.

Most notable was the prolific work of the photographer Edward S. Curtis which included beautifully conceived portraits of Indians from a large number of tribes, and scenes of daily life, which bear testimony to a way of life in decline.

Perhaps the most enduring symbol of Indian 'identity' is the ubiquitous eagle feather warbonnet. Buffalo Bill Cody's 'Wild West' tours of North America, Britain and Europe in the late nineteenth and early twentieth centuries, quickly gave rise to the popular misconception that all Native American groups wore this type of headdress, although it was largely the preserve of the Plains peoples. This stereotype of the Plains warrior became synonymous with American Indian culture in general and persists to the present day.

A huge range of novelties was produced from the early twentieth century onwards, reflecting the appeal of this stereotype in the European consciousness. One of the most popular of these was the picture postcard, most often depicting Indians in their traditional dress. Indian people themselves, understanding the exotic appeal of their cultures to non-Indians, began producing a diversity of souvenirs depicting stereotypical images of warbonnet-wearing chiefs and other Indian subjects.

From the end of the First World War onwards, and with the advent of moving pictures, the Hollywood film industry began to represent Plains Indians and the history of the West in countless western movies. Often using white actors rather than Indians, these portrayals were invariably negative in nature and seldom rose above the level of caricature. To compound the insult, it assured the stereotype would reach a mass audience.

The 1960s, however, saw a growing awareness among whites and Indians alike of the wrongs perpetrated against indigenous cultures. With the combined influence of emerging radical Native American groups, such as the American Indian Movement (AIM), certain mainstream films portrayed a more sympathetic view of Native Americans and an infinitely more accurate account of the history of the West. Films like *Soldier Blue* (1970) and *Little Big Man* (1970) challenged the commonly held prejudices. But, despite this apparent progress, fanciful depictions of Native Americans persist. In more recent years, productions such as Kevin Kostner's *Dances with Wolves* (1990)—despite its liberal credentials—still managed to project an excessively saccharine image of buffalo hunters on the Plains.

The romantic perception of the Native American's colorful past has persisted to the present day and, not for the first time, has turned Indians into a very marketable 'commodity'.

Travel brochures use a myriad of colorful images of craggy-featured, feather-bedecked chiefs, set against backdrops of snow-capped mountains and vast rolling prairies, to advertise vacations in the US and Canada. A plethora of consumer products in high street stores and shopping malls around the world reflects an international demand in post-industrial society for images and objects relating to this people who continue to represent dignity and a respect for the environment. This imagery—the Indian as dignified keeper of the land—forms part of the mythology of the American West that is difficult to differentiate from fact. It seemingly helps fill a spiritual vacuum left by the ravages of consumerism and globalization.

At the beginning of the twenty-first century, Native American culture survives. It is alive, vibrant and continually evolving—despite broken treaties and promises, corruption, alcoholism, poverty and suicide. Yet the image of the old 'Hollywood Indian' refuses to go away.

Engraving, *Indian Scalping his Dead Enemy*, late nineteenth century

Formerly benign attitudes towards Indians changed for the worse in the mid-nineteenth century as the Euro-American advance into Indian territories gathered pace and the indigenous populations retaliated against the violation of their lands. Indians were described and depicted as marauding, bloodthirsty savages, as this image illustrates.

Stereoscopic slide, T. W. Ingersoll, circa 1897-1898

This stereoscopic slide depicts a relatively harmonious scene - according to the caption, it shows Indian women drying fish. This is unlikely, of course, as the Sioux traditionally were not fish but meat eaters. It is typical of the exotic type of image of Indian people that was popular in both America and Europe in the late nineteenth and early twentieth century.

INDIAN SCALPING HIS DEAD ENEMY.

495. Drying Fish Meat in a Sioux Camp.

Sepiatone photograph, unknown photographer, circa 1900

To meet the increasing late nineteenth century demand for exotic images of Native Americans, it was common practice for studio photographers to depict Indians using wholly inappropriate props and incongruous settings. The resulting images were often of dubious authenticity, their subjects exhibiting painful embarrassment and indignity.

This example shows a young boy in Northern Plains or Plateau attire against a plain backdrop. He gazes uncomfortably down the photographer's lens, his wool leggings inexplicably arranged around his ankles. The gun and turkey feather protruding from his metal armband were almost certainly added at the photographer's suggestion.

Sepiatone photograph, unknown photographer, circa 1900

This photograph shows a group of Northern Plains men ready to participate in a dance. This was a common sight on Plains Indian reservations at the end of the nineteenth century. The two men on the left stand in set poses, one holding aloft a bow and arrow, the other with a pistol pointed at the singers seated around the dance drum. This incongruous detail was doubtless a whim of the photographer.

Chief Hiawatha,

INDIAN NOVELTIES A SPECIALITY.

·:·:·:·:·:·

GRAND RIVER RESERVATION. SIX NATIONS. ONTARIO.

CANADA.

Postcards, early 20th century

Literally thousands of souvenir postcards were produced in the early decades of the twentieth century. They depicted American Indians with varying degrees of authenticity. Warbonnet-wearing chiefs were a favorite subject.

The postcard at **top left** promotes a lecture tour by Chief Oskenonton, a Mohawk opera singer who toured Britain in the 1930s. Both he and the dubiously named 'Hiawatha', **(top center)**, are depicted dressed in eagle feather warbonnets, although this form of headgear was not traditional among their people, but regarded as a general symbol of Indian identity.

The third card **(top right)** is inaccurately colored, with added 'war paint' to enhance the exotic appeal of the subject. In the Edwardian era, 'Hiawatha' pageants were popular, inspired by Longfellow's epic poem based on Great Lakes Indian folklore. The sepiatone postcard at **bottom left** dates circa 1905 and shows young actors dressed in fanciful 'Indian' style costume, probably from a dressing-up box. They appear to be participating in an amateur performance of the Hiawatha legend, and are dressed as Hiawatha and his mother, Nokomis.

The card at **bottom right**, although depicting a Sioux Indian in a warbonnet, bears a quotation from 'The Song of Hiawatha'. This confusion between Plains and Great Lakes tribes was a common occurrence in early twentieth century literature.

" On his head his eagle feathers,
Round his waist his belt of wampum. '
"The Song of Hiawatha."—Longfellow.

Photo. Cavendish Morton.

The Warbonnet as a Symbol of American Indian Identity

Dissected puzzle, circa 1905

This Edwardian children's jigsaw puzzle depicts a strange scene of feather-bedecked Indians seated by a campfire, engaged in the most English of habits—drinking tea! Their clothing, including trailer warbonnet, is inaccurately represented, resembling children's dressing-up costumes of the period.

Parasol handle, circa 1920

This curious parasol handle is made of an early molded plastic, possibly caseine. The fanciful representation of an Indian wearing feathered warbonnet reflects the widespread post-Edwardian idea of Native Americans as objects of ridicule. Again, the warbonnet closely resembles headdresses available as children's dressing-up costumes in the early twentieth century. The rows of circles on the figure's chest, although resembling buttons, probably derive from the mirror-decorated otter fur breastplates commonly worn by the Sioux, doubtless copied from contemporary 'Wild West' images.

Alan C. Mitchell Collection

Indian chief plaque, 1960s

Made by Bosson's, chalk ware manufacturers from Congleton, England, this hand-painted plaster ornament epitomizes the eternal fondness for the image of the warbonnet-wearing Indian chief. The stoical pose with folded arms is reminiscent of the way in which Indians were commonly represented in Hollywood western movies!

Quilled box, Great Lakes region

Alan C. Mitchell Collection

Photograph album with pokerwork decoration to cover.

Souvenirs, Canada, 1920s and 30s

The image of the Plains Indian wearing eagle feather warbonnet was so prevalent that Indian people from other regions, understanding its exotic appeal, eventually adopted it themselves. Following the decline of the fur trade, this proved to be sound marketing strategy as Indian groups sought to support themselves. These items, all depicting stereotypical images of warbonnet-wearing Indians, were made for sale to early tourists in Canada in the 1920s and 30s.

Wooden pipe bowl

Lady's flat bag, Plateau, 1920s (below)

The warbonnet eventually came to be adopted by tribes other than Plains groups. To many, it was seen as the very emblem of 'Indianness'.

This beautifully beaded lady's handbag, called a flat bag, was made by one of the western Plateau groups and was carried at parades and other ceremonial occasions. One side depicts a warbonnet-wearing chief, the other a woman in Plateau style regalia. The Plateau groups were heavily influenced by Plains styles of clothing and accouterments.

Alan C. Mitchell Collection

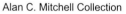

Children's Toys and Games

Doll, 1930s (right)

Indian curios were in great demand throughout the nineteenth century and well into the twentieth. This doll, dating from the 1930s, is of commercial European type and has been dressed in 'Indian' clothing, probably by Indian people in the northeastern United States, and sold as a souvenir.

Alan C. Mitchell Collection

'Swappet' toy figures (below)

These children's molded plastic action toys were made in England and Hong Kong during the 1960s. They reflect the influence of Hollywood western movies and formed part of every child's 'Cowboys and Indians' fantasy. Earlier in the century, similar toy figures were made of lead.

Doll, 1960s (above)

Commercially produced dolls of this type have been sold as cheap souvenirs since at least the 1960s. The label, which reads 'Made in the land where Hiawatha hunted', is slightly misleading. Imported from the Far East, many of these dolls were dressed by Indians as a means of supplementing their income on reservations. This doll was marketed by the famous Fred Harvey Company and sold at one of their retail outlets in the American Southwest.

Chief Cherokee doll, 1965 (right)

An Indian version of the popular 'action man' model, this toy figure was made by Louis Marx Inc. It came furnished with a range of accessories including warbonnet with detachable trailer, shield, drum, lance, bow, quiver and arrows.

Totem pole souvenirs, 1960s

These souvenir totem poles, also sold by the Fred Harvey Company, were made by Sioux Indians in the 1960s. Totem poles, of course, were not traditional to the Sioux or any other Plains Indian group. They have been made to appeal to tourists, who perhaps recognize the totem pole as a general symbol of Indian culture.

Model tipi, 1960s

This toy model tipi, produced in England by Britain's Ltd in the 1960s, is unusually accurate in construction, though the decoration is less authentically represented.

Indians In Children's Books

Grey Owl, an early Indian 'wanabee'

Archie Belaney, born in Sussex, England in 1888, became obsessed with American Indians from an early age. He

eventually emigrated to Canada, settled among Ojibwa Indians in northern Ontario, called himself 'Grey Owl' and claimed to be of mixed Indian and Scottish parentage. He wrote several books on the Canadian wilderness and, hair in braids and dressed in buckskins, toured England to promote them in the 1930s. Only after his death in 1938 was it realized that Grey Owl was an Englishman and not a Native American. Often photographed wearing a Plains style warbonnet, he was an early Indian *wanabee*.

Children's books, 1960s

The majority of publications available to children in the 1950s and 60s portray Native Americans history and culture in the most simplistic of terms. Illustrations tend to depict Native American clothing with scant regard for accuracy. In many cases, Indians are represented as mere caricatures.

'My Indian Library' set, 1960s

This series of educational books, first published in 1935, was still available to young children in the United States in the 1960s. For their time, they are quite informative.

Indians in Packaging

Box of *Redskin* gun pellets, probably 1950s

Images of Native Americans have been popularly used in marketing throughout the twentieth century to sell commodities as diverse as gambling machines, grindstones, tobacco, and camper vans. The precise nature of the association with Native Americans is not always plain to see. Presumably, in the case of this box of gun pellets, the intended reference is to the part that guns had to play in the story of the American West!

The term *redskin*, offensive to modern-day Native Americans, was familiar to all those weaned on dime novels and Hollywood westerns.

Alan C. Mitchell Collection

Indians on Coins and Stamps

Indian head cent (left)

Indians appeared on a number of United States coins and postage stamps, reflecting their popular appeal and symbolic potency. The 'Indian head cent' was designed by James Barton Longacre and was produced by the US Mint as early as 1859. The warbonnet-wearing Native American profiled bust, however, looks very European, and rumor has it that the engraver used his daughter as a model for the likeness.

Buffalo nickel (center)

The 'buffalo nickel', designed in 1911 by James Earle Fraser, was based on photographic portraits of three Plains Indian chiefs—Iron Tail, Big Tree and Two Moons. The design for the reverse of the coin was modeled from a buffalo called Black Diamond in New York's Bronx Zoo. The coin was produced from 1913 to 1938.

Sacajawea dollar (right)

The 'Sacajawea dollar' was the first new coin of the millennium. The obverse depicts Sacajawea, the Shoshone woman who, between 1804-6, guided the adventurers, Lewis and Clark, from the northern Great Plains to the Pacific Ocean and back. The coin was designed by Glenna Goodacre, and first appeared in January 2000.

Postage stamps

These postage stamps reflect the general appeal of Plains Indian culture. Particularly popular themes are prominent chiefs and the eagle feather warbonnet.

Indians in Fashion

Indian style beaded medallion necklaces, Taiwan, 1960s

These beaded necklaces were commercially made in imitation of Native American beadwork, probably in the Far East. Indian style fashion beadwork jewelry was popular among hippies in the 1960s. Much of it is machine-made rather than handcrafted. It is a poor imitation of genuine Native American work.

Alan C. Mitchell Collection

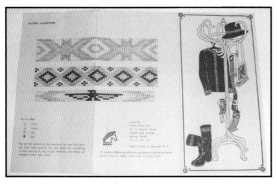

Leaflet for a bead kit, 1960s

American Indian style beadwork kits, including bead loom and instructions, were popular for many decades in the United States and Europe. This instruction leaflet describes how to make loomed beadwork in typical Indian designs. It dates from the 1960s, when Indian-style fashion accessories were in vogue.

Alan C. Mitchell Collection

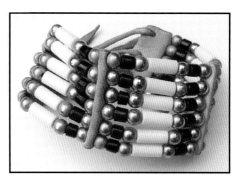

Wristband, 1992

Indian style fashion accessories are a recurrent presence in the high street. Imported beadwork jewelry, fringed leather bags and footwear, tubular bead chokers and other novelties are just a few examples of this trend. This wristband, although Indian-made, is typical of the sort of mass-produced fashion jewelry popular in worldwide high street fashion stores over the last few years.

End of the Trail belt buckle, 1990 (below)

The image of the Plains warrior, bent over his weary war pony, is inspired by a sculpture by James Earle Fraser, designer of the 'buffalo nickel'. The original statue was created for the 1915 Panama-Pacific International Exhibition in San Francisco. By this time, Indians were regarded as part of the past, a vanishing race, with no part to play in the twentieth century.

The image is regarded by many modern-day Native Americans as a reminder of defeat and subjugation a century ago. Even today, however, it is widely reproduced in the form of postcards, prints and curios, to sell the legend of the conquest of the American West.

Courtesy of Moose Wells

Indians in Cinema

Film still, *Indian Agent*, 1948

Hollywood western movies gained in popularity from the end of the First World War until the 1960s. They told the story of the inevitable clash of worlds of the Indian and the white man. Indians, however, were generally depicted in an extremely negative and simplistic manner. This film still shows the celebrated 'Indian' movie actor Iron Eyes Cody (right) in the 1948 film *Indian Agent*.

Cody is familiar to many for his portrayal of the tear-shedding Indian in an environmental campaign televised in the United States in the 1970s. After appearing in dozens of Hollywood westerns, the earliest in 1919, he turned out to be of Sicilian extraction and not Native American.

RKO Pictures. Courtesy of Marsh & Marsh Ltd.

Dances with Wolves video, 1990

The film *Dances With Wolves*, released in 1990, presented a positive, if somewhat romanticized, picture of the Sioux. It was notable for using a full cast of Native American actors, using Lakota language, with subtitles in English. Its portrayal of the Sioux's enemies, the Pawnee, however, proved as superficial as the earlier Hollywood depictions of 'bloodthirsty savages'.

Orion Films

Indians and the Travel Industry

Colorful images of Indians have been used for many decades to entice travelers to visit North America and its 'exotic' peoples and places. Proud Plains Indian chiefs wearing warbonnets are favorite subjects.

Calendar, 2004

Images of contemporary Indians in their exuberant pow wow regalia prove as exotic in their appeal as those of the old-time chiefs. Their faces grace an enormous range of posters, book covers, greeting cards, calendars, postcards, CDs, bookmarks and T-shirts.

Ben Marra 2004 Calendar

DISKY Communications, Europe B.V.

Indians and New Age culture

Badges, 1970s (below left)

The 1970s saw a number of protests by militant groups such as the American Indian Movement (AIM). This increased awareness of Indian struggles for improved education, health, sanitation and employment on Indian reservations, as well as the publication of books like Dee Brown's *Bury My Heart at Wounded Knee*, led to renewed and widespread interest in Native American history and culture. These badges of prominent Plains chiefs, Young-Man-Afraid-of-his-Horses, Standing Bear, and Washakie, illustrate the new cult status of Native American leaders in the consciousness of post-industrial urban cultures.

Native American style music CD, 1997 (above right)

Urban cultures have always romanticized tribal peoples. This New Age music CD, although purporting to be of authentic Native American songs, is actually a reworked, synthesized version, more palatable to western European taste.

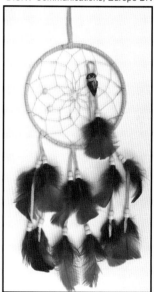

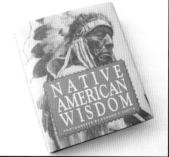

'Native American Wisdom' book, 1994 (above right)

This small book of quotations emphasizing the Native American's respect for the Earth, is typical of the sort of material produced in the wake of the film *Dances With Wolves*, when Native American culture once again became all the rage. It illustrates the way in which the Indian epitomizes wisdom and ecological awareness. The myth of the Noble Savage is a consistently marketable commodity!

Resin model Indian, circa 2000 (right)

This cast resin model was imported from China in the last few years. It is a crude stereotype of a cross-legged Indian chief, the warbonnet and clothing inaccurately represented.

Dream catcher, 1999 (above)

The "Dream catcher", although an authentic Native American object, has become a universal ornament. Often made and sold by non-Indians, it exemplifies the trend for New Age culture and a quest for spiritual values in a consumer society.

Nico Strange Owl with her son Dah'som (Northern Cheyenne).
Photo courtesy of Eagle Plume's
Allenspark, Colorado USA
Photograph by www.milnephotography.com

At one point we were sedentary farmers, and it was during this time that corn became an important element in our ceremonial ways. As we moved further westward [onto the Plains] and adapted to the horse culture, our leaders put those sedentary ways to rest and moved forward. But corn still is very important to us. We are strengthened by our history and the knowledge that we can adapt.

- Nico Strange Owl, Northern Cheyenne (March 2004)

The Catalog

The Warrior's World
Weapons

CHANGING WORLDS

The late nineteenth century was a period of great change in Plains Indian life. In terms of material culture, this was particularly the case. Weapon-making skills did not decline completely with the passing of the buffalo days. Stone-headed clubs, tomahawks, shields, sinew-backed bows and other weapons continued to be made, although their form and their meaning often altered in accordance with the enforced sedentary lifestyle imposed upon these formerly nomadic peoples.

Clubs

War clubs with carefully fashioned stone heads were traditional fighting weapons among Plains peoples. Sometimes known as 'skull crackers', for obvious reasons, the earliest clubs were very sturdily made and rather plain. Late nineteenth century examples were sometimes embellished with beaded, quilled or plaited horsehair wrapping.

The stone head, often a kind of soapstone, was held in position by means of a sturdy rawhide strap that was an extension of the hide-wrapped handle. It was further secured by means of a shallow hole at the center of the head. Stone heads on nineteenth century and later examples tend to be ovoid, with pointed ends.

During the reservation period, the Plains tribes continued to make this type of stone-headed club for ceremonial use. From the late nineteenth century onwards, large numbers were also made for sale, particularly by the Sioux. These later examples were generally flimsier versions of the original weapons of combat. They have a much deeper hole into which the stone head is fixed into position, and a narrower band of rawhide over the head.

Some clubs made for the curio market were decorated with 'salt and pepper' beading, leftover beads being mixed randomly and spiral-wrapped around the club's shaft. Many examples have long suspensions of dyed horsehair to the end of the shaft, among other forms of embellishment.

Another type of club used by various Plains groups is the 'slingshot' club with flail type head. In the early twentieth century, certain Northern groups made highly embellished versions of these weapons for ceremonial use and for sale. Many of these have bead-wrapped handles and fully-beaded stone heads.

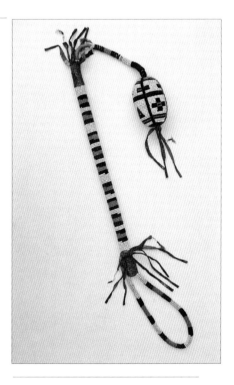

Slingshot club, Northern Plains, circa 1920-30

Wood, stone, native leather, textile, metal cones
Length, excluding hide fringe, 80 cm

This slingshot type club is probably Stoney-Assiniboine. The ovoid stone head is fully covered in couched overlay beadwork. The entire shaft, connecting thong and loop handle are also fully bead-wrapped. Beads are of Czech type. Note the tin cone jingles suspended from the smoked hide fringe at the top of the stone head.

Slingshot clubs of this type were commonly made for sale to early visitors to the Canadian Rockies area. Some examples substitute a hard rubber ball for the stone flail head.

Slingshot club, Northern Plains, circa 1910
Wood, stone, glass beads, buckskin, textile, feathers, pigment
Length, excluding beaded tab and feathers, 58 cm

This ceremonial club was probably made by one of the Blackfoot or Stoney-Assiniboine groups of southern Alberta. It was collected by the Reverend A.W. MacMichael between 1914-20 while working as Head of the South Alberta Mission in Edmonton. During this time, MacMichael amassed a substantial collection of Northern Plains objects. He later returned to England to act as chaplain to the Archbishop of Canterbury.

The example illustrated here has a small spherical stone head, encased in brain-tanned buckskin and stained with red pigment, with two eagle feathers attached. The shaft is wrapped with beads in bands of dark blue, dark green, white and amber. The fringed triangular tab at the opposite end is decorated with a stacked arrangement of geometric designs in couched overlay technique.

A similar slingshot war club was collected by the English collector, James Hooper.
[Phelps, 1975: plate 212; p.352, no.1690].

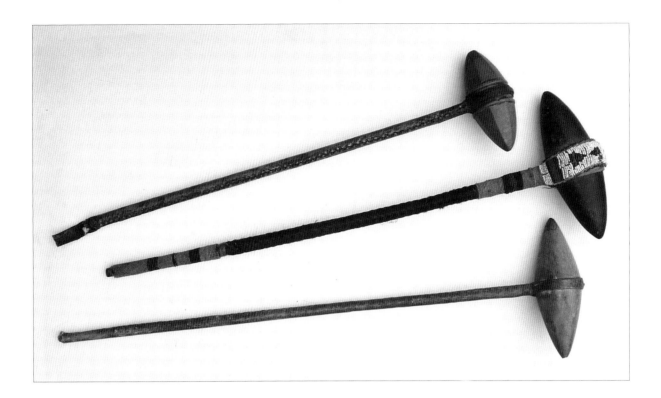

War club, Plains, circa 1860-80 *(top)*
Stone, wood, rawhide, sinew
Length 63.5 cm, width of head 14 cm

This club was probably made as a weapon rather than for ceremonial use. The soapstone head is beautifully faceted, the center part carved with raised rings. The shaft is encased in thick buffalo rawhide, and shows evidence of having once been spirally wrapped with narrow bands of porcupine quillwork. It once belonged to the English collector and historian, E.H. Blackmore.

War club, Central Plains, probably Sioux, circa 1880 *(center)*
Stone, wood, glass beads, rawhide, buckskin, textile, horsehair, sinew
Length 66 cm, width of head 19 cm

The large head of this club is made of a dark gray-colored stone. The handle is wrapped with seed beads and black horsehair plaiting, a specialty of the Sioux. Around the head is a secondary buckskin strap, decorated with two lanes of lane-stitch beadwork. The sturdy construction possibly suggests use as a weapon rather than for ceremonial purposes.

War club, Plains, circa 1900 *(bottom)*
Stone, wood, rawhide, sinew, pigment
Length 69 cm, width of head 17.5 cm

This club is of relatively lightweight construction, and was probably made for sale. The Sioux must have made thousands of this type for the curio market in the late nineteenth century and first decades of the twentieth. The rawhide shaft has been rubbed with red earth pigment. A vestige of sinew attached to the top of the head probably served to attach an appendage such as a feather.

Pipe-tomahawk, Plains, circa 1860-80 *(right)*

Iron, wood
Length 68.5, width of head 24.5 cm

The 'spontoon' tomahawk is of eighteenth century French origin. Its distinctive diamond-shaped blade resembled a military pole-axe called an *esponton,* used by French commissioned officers.

The most common type of spontoon tomahawk incorporated a pipe bowl. The pierced lobes seen on this example have replaced the 'basal processes' which are a feature of many earlier specimens. Many of these spontoon pipe-tomahawks were made in France until the late nineteenth century, although others were produced in England and America. The long, tapered ash wood haft is undrilled.

A similar specimen, illustrated by Peterson [1965: no. 287], was reportedly owned by the Kiowa war leader, Kicking Bird.

Pipe-tomahawk, Northern Plains, circa 1910-15 *(left)*

Pewter, wood, fur, glass beads, native leather, cotton thread
Length, excluding beaded tab, 40 cm, width of head 24.5 cm

This Northern Plains pipe-tomahawk, of early twentieth century vintage, probably originates from the Blackfoot or Stoney of southern Alberta. Its function is as a showy ceremonial accessory, not a weapon. Note the large pewter blade with diminutive bowl, and the beaver fur-wrapped handle. The triangular beaded pendant is decorated with stacked geometric designs in couched overlay technique within a single-lane border of lane-stitch, with long buckskin fringe below. The haft is undrilled.

[Peterson, 1965: nos. 247-9]

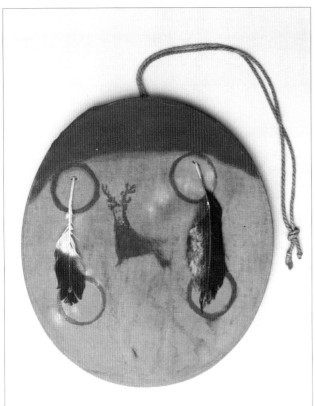 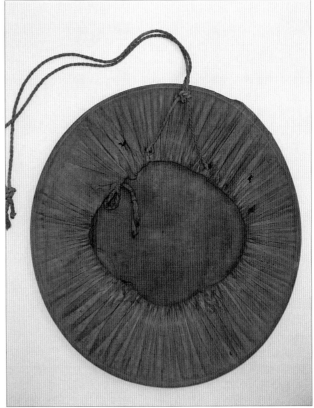

Shield, Central Plains, Teton Sioux, circa 1880-1900

Muslin, wood, paint, eagle feathers
Diameter (maximum) 43 cm

By the late nineteenth century, the need for thick rawhide shields as protection in battle was but a memory. Instead, more lightweight shields became fashionable, made of muslin stretched over a wooden hoop and bearing symbolic designs personal to the owner. This development illustrates the inherent protective power of Plains shield *design* rather than its value in deflecting enemies' weapons.

This painted muslin shield was made by the Oglala Sioux chief, Iron Tail (Sinte Maza), who worked for several years with William Cody and his 'Wild West' in the early years of the twentieth century. It was given by him to Fred B. Hackett of Chicago who, in earlier years, was a ration clerk with the Oglala Sioux agency at Pine Ridge, South Dakota, and between 1914-17 worked for Cody, chasing Indians around the arena in rough-riding exhibitions. He managed the Sioux recruits to the touring show and became a close friend of the Sioux chief, eventually being adopted as his son. On Iron Tail's death in 1916, Hackett was responsible for his funeral arrangements at Holy Rosary, Pine Ridge.

The designs painted on the shield, featuring the figure of an elk within an arrangement of four circular devices, suggest that Iron Tail may have been a member of the Elk Dreamer Society. The male elk was considered by the Sioux to have special powers over courtship, and these powers, it was believed, were transferred to men who dreamt of this animal. The four circles probably had some protective function. [Wissler, 1907: 25 (fig.2), 40], possibly representing the hoops carried by Elk Dreamers [Wissler, 1907: 42]. Another interesting element of the composition, commonly seen on Sioux shields, is the arc of deep red at the top of the design, which may be a representation of spiritual power from the sky.

Gun case, Northern Plains, Gros Ventre, circa 1910

Native leather, glass beads, woolen cloth, cotton thread
Length, excluding fringe, 101 cm, width 15 cm

This gun case, probably made at Fort Belknap reservation, Montana, was collected around 1920 by Royal Canadian Mounted Police (RCMP) Officer Brace. Brace was an avid gun collector and later became a Canadian MP.

Constructed of brain-tanned hide, each end is decorated with a panel of geometric couched overlay beadwork within lane-stitch borders. The simple hourglass designs are beaded on the hide first and the medium blue background filled in afterwards.

Gun cases continued to be made by Northern Plains tribes well after the buffalo days were ended and were popular ceremonial accessories, carried by well-dressed men at celebrations and in horseback parades.

Ceremonial lance, Northern Plains, circa 1900-10

Wood, glass beads, textile, antler, native leather, feathers, horsehair
Maximum length 112 cm

This interesting type of decorated lance, originating from one of the Northern Plains peoples of Alberta, dates from the first decade of the twentieth century. Judging by the extent of its decoration, it appears to be a ceremonial item of a type used for parades such as Banff Indian Days and Calgary Stampede. These events attracted large crowds of inquisitive non-Native onlookers, many of them early tourist visitors who arrived in the Canadian Rockies via the Canadian Pacific Railroad. Decorated staffs and lances seem to have been particularly favored by the Stoneys in the early twentieth century.

Photos by David Rowan

The lance is quite short in length, its style possibly emulating the Canadian Mounted Police lance as much as a nostalgic reference to the old warrior days. It was collected by a chaplain to the Archbishop of Canterbury while working with a mission in Alberta between 1914-20, and was purchased from his clergy family descendants in Faversham, Kent, England.

The entire shaft has been wrapped along its length with a floral patterned cotton cloth. The majority of the length is tightly spiral-wrapped in glass seed beads of various colors.

At the tip of the lance is a carefully fashioned point made of elk antler, finely thinned, shaped and polished, and set into the end of the shaft. The length of the shaft is wrapped with seed beads in bands of color, further embellished with short projecting tufts of black horsehair, neatly trimmed to a uniform length, and short buckskin fringes. Attached to one of the fringes are two red-tailed hawk tail feathers, the base of the quills removed and each cut down to 14 cm in length.

At the end of the handle is attached an interesting variety of ornaments. Firstly, a narrow strap, fully beaded in couched overlay technique with a repeated cross motif in white-core red and translucent dark green on a periwinkle blue ground, commercial thread-sewn and couched. Secondly, a further strap consisting of two identical bead-wrapped cloth rolls, in translucent navy blue and chalk white beads. The two beaded rolls are stitched together at intervals, not separate. The final detail consists of a rattle, made of a circular tin container, probably for old-fashioned shoe buttons. The whole tin is encased in buckskin, and one half of each side painted in green earth pigment, the other in red.

The Warrior's World
Clothing

CHANGING STYLES

The influence of imported trade materials upon traditional Plains cultures in the nineteenth century was enormous. Various types of woolen and cotton cloth, much of which was manufactured in the northern English textile mills, were utilized by Indians for clothing and ceremonial items. Brass bells, thimbles, brass and nickel buttons, and dome-headed upholstery tacks were all used to decorative effect on a wide range of traditional objects. Glass trade beads from Europe revolutionized Plains Indian artistic traditions, probably more so than any other imported item.

By the turn of the century, the importance of the old warrior societies and the battle honors system was rapidly disintegrating as a result of drastically changing cultural circumstances, and the context of traditional clothing and ceremonial paraphernalia was in the process of evolving accordingly. (See chapter, *Behold These Things.*)

MR. BALDWIN BECOMES "BIG CHIEF SITTING EAGLE," OF THE STONEY TRIBE : THE PRIME MINISTER IN HIS FEATHERED HEAD-DRESS ; WITH MRS. BALDWIN AND CHIEF SITTING EAGLE AND HIS SQUAW.

Chief Sitting Eagle (left) of the Chiniki band of Stoneys, and the Rt. Hon. Stanley Baldwin, after the British prime minister's investiture as honorary chief at Banff Springs Hotel, Banff, Alberta on 12 August 1927. Baldwin wears the double trailer warbonnet presented to him by Sitting Eagle, together with the shirt and leggings illustrated on pages 90 and 91. The photograph was taken by W.J. Oliver, staff photographer for the Calgary Herald.

Shirt, Northern Plains, Stoney-Assiniboine, circa 1920
Native leather, glass beads, canvas
Overall length 85 cm

The twentieth century brought many changes to men's traditional regalia. Hide shirts became much more tailored in cut. With the decrease in the importance of warrior societies and their associated paraphernalia, shirts were no longer stained with mineral pigments or painted with symbolic motifs, as had earlier been the case. Instead, the skin was left a natural creamy white.

This shirt, together with the pair of leggings illustrated on page 91, was presented by the Stoney chief, Sitting Eagle (John Hunter), to the British Prime Minister, Stanley Baldwin on the occasion of his investiture as honorary chief at Banff Springs Hotel on 12 August 1927.

Constructed of creamy-white buckskin, it is of typical Stoney style, with broad beaded strips in couched overlay technique, (alternatively referred to as *appliqué*, or spot stitch). The design features diagonal stripes composed of small rectangular blocks, alternating with pairs of diamonds, on a white ground. Note the low positioning of the bib to both front and back. The neckline is folded over and stitched, with a serrated edge decoration. The lower edge has a wide cut fringe, with serrations. The sleeves are similarly decorated, with pierced holes to the 'swallowtail' trim.

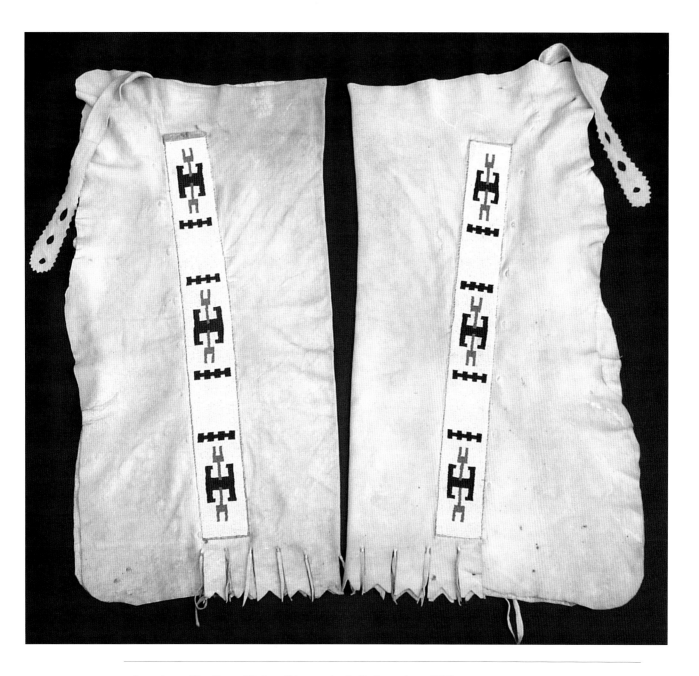

Leggings, Northern Plains, Stoney-Assiniboine, circa 1920

Native leather, glass beads, canvas
Length 80 cm

Among many Northern Plains groups, the older style of tubular hide leggings was eventually replaced by 'chap' style buckskin leggings of creamy-white buckskin, copied from cowboy work gear. This pair was presented to the Rt Hon Stanley Baldwin by Chief Sitting Eagle on the occasion of Baldwin's investiture as honorary chief of the Stoneys on 12 August 1927. Note the wide strips of couched overlay beadwork. The H-shaped motif possibly signifies the initial 'H' of the Hunter family. The outer flaps are left untrimmed, the lower edge of the hide around the ankle are cut with 'swallowtail' fringe, and the buckskin belt ties are serrated and pierced. Each legging is closed by means of buckskin laces, tied off at the back and threaded with light blue Bohemian cane beads.

Trailer warbonnet, Central Plains, Teton Sioux, circa 1910

Eagle feathers, felt, woolen cloth, glass beads, fur, native leather, metal, canvas, silk, sinew
Height 41 cm, Length 175 cm
Ex Fred Harvey and Ruth Edwards Kilgour collections

The eagle feather warbonnet was, in the nineteenth century, an important indication of a warrior's coups or military honors. By the early twentieth century, a generation of Sioux had faced up to substantial change in traditional culture. Old-time military societies and the ceremonies that accompanied them were rapidly becoming customs of a bygone era. Among many Plains peoples, however, there was widespread nostalgia for the old warrior days and, in Fourth of July parades and other celebrations, Plains peoples sought to regain the glory of former times.

As a result of the influence of Buffalo Bill Cody's touring 'Wild West' show, among other similar attractions, the concept of traditional Sioux dress became stereotyped, not only in the Euro-American consciousness but in the minds of the sons and daughters of buffalo hunters. In many respects, the warbonnet became a symbol of Indian identity, a position it seems to have occupied for a century and longer.

The Lakota word for the warbonnet is wapaha. The trailer warbonnet is referred to as wapaha iyuslohetun, or 'warbonnet that drags behind'.

This warbonnet is constructed of fifty-four immature golden eagle tail feathers, twenty-six of which are mounted on a grey felt cap, cut down from a Stetson hat. The base of each feather is decorated with pink-dyed eagle down feathers; the tip of each feather with undyed down feathers and red-dyed horsehair.

The trailer is decorated with a further twenty-eight immature golden eagle tail feathers, mounted on red woolen cloth, backed with canvas and edged with a broad orange silk ribbon. Small nickel shoe buttons provide added ornament at intervals along its length.

The browband is decorated with geometric designs in lane-stitch beadwork, sinew-sewn. To each side is a beaded rosette, with suspensions of brown fur animal tails and variously colored silk ribbons. The back of the cap is shingled with smaller eagle feathers, some dyed, and a stripped eagle primary feather.

[Kilgour, 1958: 18]

The Warrior's World
Trade Cloth Clothing

Imported woolen trade cloth called 'saved list' or 'broadcloth' revolutionized Plains material culture in the nineteenth century. The woolen fabric with its distinctive undyed white selvedge was much favored by most Plains peoples. In the case of the Sioux, it became the hallmark of the period between 1890-1925, and was used to make a wide range of items of clothing and other ceremonial accoutrements, including men's leggings, women's dresses, blankets, and warbonnet trailers. (See chapter, *Something Splendid I Wear).*

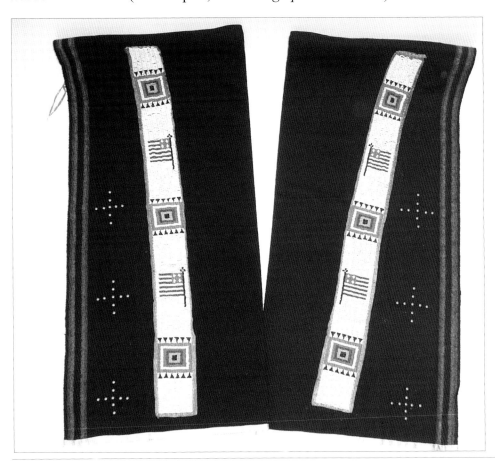

Man's leggings, probably Teton Sioux, circa 1925-35

Woolen cloth, native leather, glass beads, sinew, silk ribbon
Length 88 cm

This pair of woolen cloth leggings has beaded strips with six parallel lanes of lane-stitch beadwork, sinew-sewn on brain-tanned hide. The designs consist of U.S. flag motifs alternating with square blocks with small triangular appendages. Use of the U.S. flag became popular among the Sioux and other Plains groups towards the end of the nineteenth century, continuing well into the twentieth. The use of black beads on the beaded strips probably indicates a date around the 1920s or 30s, while the leggings of 'rainbow' selvedge cloth were made for the author by a Sioux friend at Pine Ridge, South Dakota in the late 1980s.

Man's leggings, Teton Sioux, circa 1890

Woolen cloth, native leather, glass beads, sinew, cotton
Length 81 cm

Trade cloth leggings of this type became extremely popular with the Sioux and other Plains groups in the second half of the nineteenth century. Their simple construction was copied from American-European buckskin 'chap' style leggings of the period.

This pair is constructed of navy blue saved list cloth, the undyed selvedge running vertically up the outer edge of the front of each legging. The remaining edges of the cloth are bound with a floral-patterned cotton fabric. The beaded strips are decorated with six parallel lanes of lane-stitch beadwork, sinew-sewn on buckskin. The design features alternating steep-sided triangles with internal elaboration, and crosses in transparent dark blue, white-core rose and medium green on a white ground. To the center of each of the crosses is a small block of faceted brass beads.

The leggings are from the collection of Clarance Hortover, who amassed a collection of Plains material in the first half of the twentieth century while traveling throughout the United States, working in the field of energy products. During this time he befriended many Indians and established his 'Museum of the Kentucky Rifle and the American Indian' in Newholland, Pennsylvania in the 1920s. The collection was dispersed in the 1980s.

Trade cloth leggings continue to be made by the modern-day Sioux as part of traditional dance regalia, and have altered very little in design. Since the disappearance of the old undyed selvedge cloth, however, the edges tend to be bound with colored edging cloth. Reproduction saved list cloth is also now available.

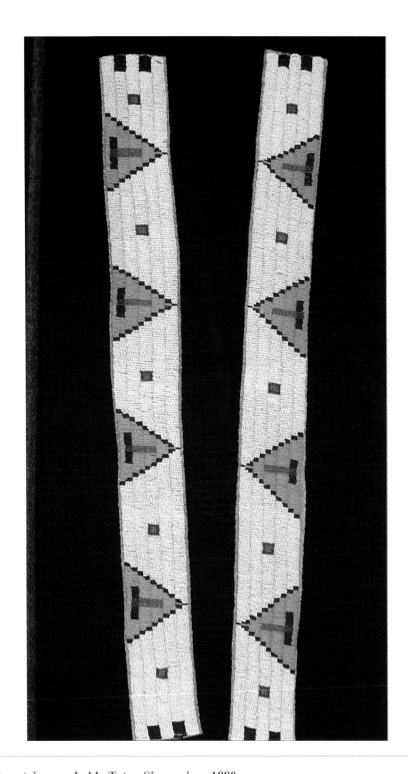

Man's legging strips, probably Teton Sioux, circa 1880

Native leather, glass beads, sinew
Length (each) 63 cm

This pair of beaded legging strips is executed in lane-stitch, five lanes in width. The design of repeated triangles is slightly unusual in its use of predominantly greasy yellow beads. To the reverse of each strip is a series of parallel lines in red earth pigment, possibly indicating they were once attached to a pair of hide leggings with painted horizontal stripes.

Breechcloth, Plateau, Nez Percé, circa 1910-20

Woolen cloth, glass beads, cotton thread, silk ribbon, metal sequins
Length 131 cm

Woolen trade cloth with undyed selvedge was widely used by all Plains and Plateau groups. This breechcloth was collected from the Lawyer family. Chief Lawyer was a well-known Nez Percé leader at the time of the treaty of 1855. The breechcloth is applied with parallel bands of lane-stitch in size 13/0 Czech beads.

A Warrior I Have Been

Aprons, Southern Plains, Oto, circa 1910-20

Woolen cloth, glass beads, cotton thread, silk ribbon
Length (each) 63 cm

The woolen cloth used to make this pair of aprons is of the mohair 'rainbow' selvedge type, extremely popular among many Southern Plains and Prairie tribes. Each apron is decorated with a different composition of white-outlined, stylized semi-floral designs in couched overlay technique, a style much favored by the Oto and other Oklahoma groups. They probably started life as a breechcloth and at some stage were cut in half or had a section cut from the middle. They came from the Lola Lawrence Collection of Oklahoma City, Oklahoma.

Blanket, Central Plains, probably Cheyenne, circa 1880

Woolen cloth, native leather, glass and metal beads, sinew, cotton thread
Length 216 cm, width 158 cm

Woolen blankets with beaded strips are commonly seen in old photographs of Sioux men in traditional dress. They enjoyed particular popularity in the period between the late 1880s and 1925 when large numbers of Sioux were recruited to participate in the various 'wild west' shows, including those organized by William Cody and Pawnee Bill.

Large blankets of this kind were sometimes called 'courting blankets' and were fashionable among the Sioux, Cheyenne and Arapaho. They were made of a large piece of woolen trade cloth, or from two pieces stitched together with a seam in the middle. The use of decorated strips on woolen blankets dates back to an earlier practice of applying quillwork bands to buffalo robes. These covered a seam where the two halves of a hide were stitched back together after tanning, and may have represented the animal's backbone.

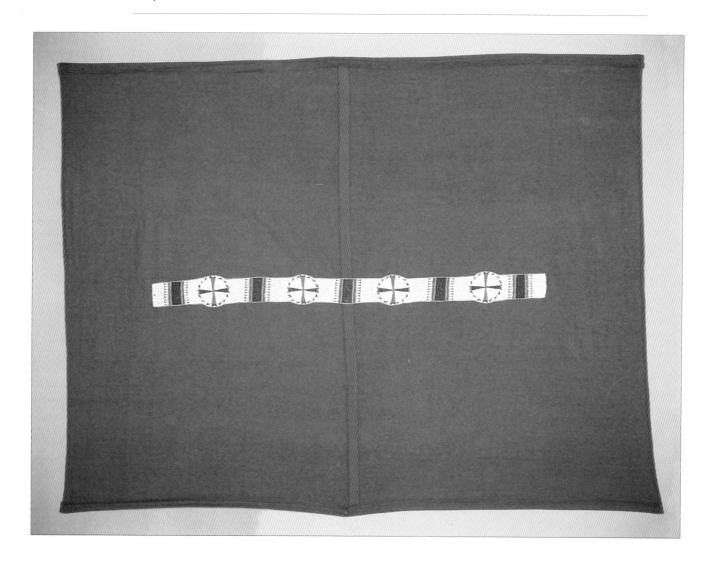

Blanket strip, Northern Plains, probably Stoney-Assiniboine, circa 1920-40

Canvas, glass beads, native leather, cotton thread
Length 92 cm, maximum width 17 cm

Wide 'stole' type blanket strips of this type were favored by many of the Northern Plains groups. These were not necessarily applied to a cloth blanket, often carried separately as a decorative accessory of traditional dress, or draped over the horse during parades. This example is probably Stoney, dating from the 1920s or 30s, and employs a range of sparkling beads. The mixture of bold geometric and floral designs is a typical Stoney trait.

The Warrior's World
Non-Native Influences

The Plains Indian trend for copying white clothing styles dates back at least to the nineteenth century. In the 1880s, for example, many Plains peoples began to make elaborately beaded versions of store-bought vests, as well as gauntlet style gloves, probably copied from military gauntlets. 'Chap' style leggings, widely adopted by the Blackfoot and other groups around the turn of the century, were based on cowboy work gear.

VESTS

The vest was not an indigenous article of clothing to Native American people. Commercially produced Euro-American style cloth vests were fashionable in white American society of the day, and were advertised in contemporary store catalogues. By the 1870s they had become incorporated into traditional native clothing, exemplifying the new mixture of white and Indian dress which occurred from the mid-nineteenth century onwards.

The eventual trend was for Indian women to make native versions of cloth vests from brain-tanned hide. Fully-beaded vests probably appeared among the Teton Sioux in the early 1880s, reaching their height of popularity during the 1890s and in the first decade of the twentieth century. Similar vests were fashionable among the Cheyenne, Arapaho and other Central Plains tribes.

Central Plains vests were beaded to front and back with lane-stitch beadwork. Arrangements of geometric designs were the vogue, *tipi and clouds* motifs being a favorite choice, with *meat rack* devices positioned along the lower edge of the composition (right). Some beaded vests from this area were decorated with U.S. flags and representational designs, based on pictographic drawings of war exploits. These designs included animals, human figures and mounted horsemen.

Further north, the Canadian Plains groups were making their own versions of bead-decorated vests. The Blackfoot, Stoney-Assiniboine, Sarsi and Plains Cree all made vests with fully beaded front panels decorated in couched overlay technique. Designs consisted of simple geometric or floral compositions, usually beaded on canvas, sometimes on hide. The backs were usually of plain cloth. Similar vests also became popular with the Plateau groups.

Designs commonly used on Sioux vests

'Tipi and Clouds'

'Meat Rack'

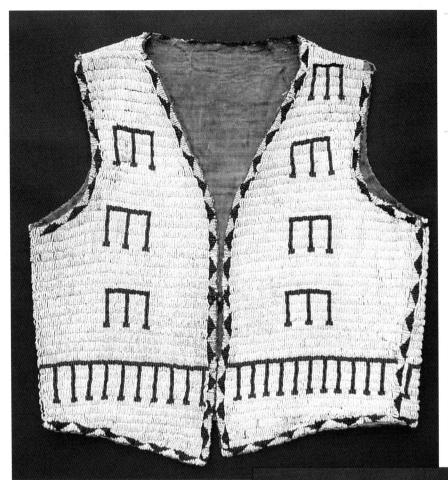

Beaded vest, Central Plains, Teton Sioux, circa 1880-90 (front and back)

Native leather, glass beads, sinew, textile
Length of back 44.5 cm

This Sioux vest belonged to Jack Eagle Eye Carson (above right), the adopted son of the 'Wild West' showman, Texas Jack Omohundro. Carson, who claimed Cherokee descent, also worked as a Wild West show performer, and toured Britain with a traveling circus in the 1930s. He is pictured, above, wearing the Sioux vest as part of his outfit. The vest is beaded in lane-stitch technique with simple dark blue 'M'-shaped designs on a white ground, sinew-sewn. These designs obviously derive from the 'meat rack' design which is a feature of the lower edge of the beaded field. Interestingly, the design to the front shoulder is not repeated on the opposite side. This contravention of symmetrical composition appears to have been a deliberate choice on the part of the beadworker.

[Green, 1993; Green, 1997 b]

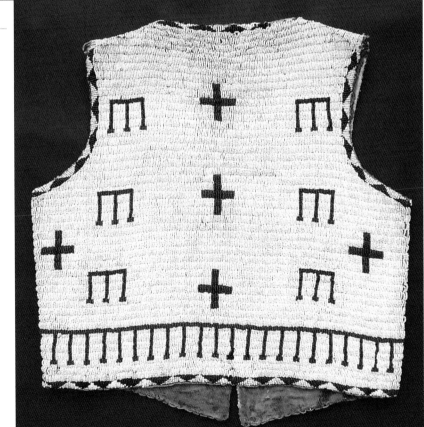

Beaded vest, Central Plains, Teton Sioux, circa 1890-1910

Native leather, glass beads, sinew
Length 55.5 cm

This vest has a particularly well-conceived composition of geometric designs in lane-stitch technique, including 'tipi and cloud' motifs and U.S. guidons and flags to both front and back, and 'meat rack' device to the lower edge of the back. The split 'tipi and cloud' designs are unusual, though occur on another vest, probably by the same maker, in the collections of the American Museum of Natural History, New York [Wissler, 1904: pl.LVI (1)].

Large quantities of beaded regalia with U.S. flag iconography were made for use in annual Fourth of July celebrations. Despite this, however, the 'Stars and Stripes' were not regarded as a particularly patriotic symbol. Well acquainted with the importance of military insignia, the Sioux adopted it as a specific emblem of Indian identity.

Beaded vest, Northern Plains, possibly Stoney-Assiniboine, circa 1900-10

Glass beads, canvas, woolen and cotton cloth
Length 59 cm

The entire front of this vest is decorated with couched overlay beadwork on canvas.
The stacked layering of geometric designs, the straight-sided hourglass designs with
small triangular appendages, and the diagonals to the shoulders, are all strong Stoney
characteristics, also shared by the neighboring Blackfoot. The back of the vest is made
of dark blue cotton cloth, lined with cream-colored cotton.

Beaded vest, Northern Plains, possibly Stoney-Assiniboine, circa 1910-20

Glass and metal beads, canvas, velvet, cotton fabric
Length 61 cm

The front of this beaded vest is fully beaded in couched overlay technique on canvas, with a lane-stitch border to the edge of the front panels. It is lined with cotton ticking. The back is of red velvet with an overall beaded diaper design. The stacked diamonds, the diagonal devices to the shoulders, and the row of small-scale diamonds to the bottom of the beaded field, are typical Stoney features.

The vest is part of a significant collection of Northern Plains material collected by the Reverend A.W. MacMichael between 1914-20 while working as Head of the South Alberta Mission in Edmonton. In 1920, he returned to England to act as chaplain to the Archbishop of Canterbury.

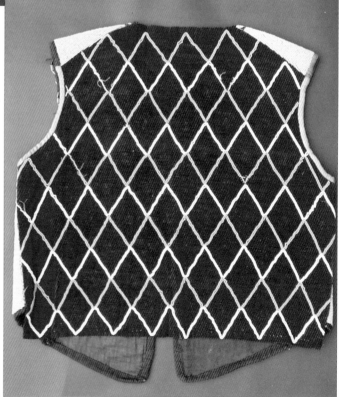

Beaded vest, Plateau, possibly Flathead, circa 1920-40

Glass beads, canvas, cotton cloth, cotton thread
Length 53 cm

The popularity of the beaded vest spread throughout the Plains, and as far west as the Plateau groups. Tribes like the Flathead, Nez Percé, Yakama, and Umatilla, although geographically distant from the Plains region, began making Plains style regalia from an early date.

This vest is finely beaded with bold floral designs in couched overlay technique. Much Plateau beadwork is executed in the tiniest sizes of beads, and workmanship was of the highest quality. Small 'cut' beads were particularly favored, creating a sparkling effect to beaded accoutrements.

Gloves, Plateau or Northern Plains, circa 1920

Native leather, glass beads, cotton fabric, cotton thread
Length (each) 39 cm

Gauntlet type gloves were copied from non-native prototypes and quickly became absorbed as part of Indian apparel among various Northern Plains, Plateau and Intermontane groups.
The fringed cuffs of this pair of gloves are beaded with a symmetrical arrangement of floral designs in couched overlay technique. They are lined with a pink and white striped cotton fabric.

Gloves, Northern Plains, Stoney-Assiniboine, circa 1910-20

Native leather, glass beads, canvas, cotton cloth, cotton thread
Length (each) 33 cm

This pair of gloves, made of white buckskin, was probably made for the souvenir trade. The cuffs are fully beaded in couched overlay with a design of stylized flowers, the background filled in diagonally in extremely small beads. Note the serrated buckskin trim around the beaded field. They were collected by the Revd A.W. MacMichael, while working as Head of the South Alberta Mission between 1914-20. During this time, MacMichael amassed a substantial collection of Northern Plains objects. He later returned to England to act as chaplain to the Archbishop of Canterbury.

Gloves, Plateau, possibly Yakama, circa 1910

Native leather, glass beads, canvas, cotton fabric, cotton thread
Length (each) 38 cm

This pair of glove gauntlets is decorated with a design of three five-petal flowers and three heart-shaped leaves, beaded in couched overlay technique on canvas. They are lined with a black floral patterned cotton cloth.

Gloves, Intermontane region, probably Crow or Flathead, circa 1930

Native leather, glass beads, cotton fabric, cotton thread
Length (each) 34 cm

This pair of gloves, probably made for a young lady, may have been made for sale. The bold floral designs in couched overlay technique, with contrasting outlines and short linear veins traced on the petals, as well as the combination of bead colors used, are typical of beadwork from groups such as the Crow, Flathead and Shoshone.

Collar and Necktie, Northern Plains, circa 1920-40

Glass beads, canvas, cotton fabric, cotton thread
Length (tie) 33 cm

One new item of men's regalia that made an appearance on the Canadian Plains in the 1920s and 30s is the beaded collar and necktie set. Countless old photographs of Blackfoot, Stoney, Plains Cree and Sarsi men in their ceremonial clothing bear testimony to its popularity.

Obviously inspired by the Euro-American shirt collar and necktie, the collar and necktie set is an example of the common Native American fondness for borrowing an idea and turning it into something new and uniquely "Indian" in flavor.

The beaded collar and tie was made either of canvas or buckskin and beaded in couched overlay technique. The majority of examples, as in this case, are made of canvas, sometimes stiffened with thick brown paper, and backed with cotton cloth. Decoration generally takes the form of either geometric or floral motifs, either on a solidly beaded or plain hide background.

This example probably originates from the Blackfoot or the Stoney, and dates somewhere between 1920 and late 1930s. The design of bold hearts in red sparkling beads on a background of medium blue Venetian beads, is rather striking. The sparkling beads are of French stock, and were particularly popular among the Canadian Plains tribes in the 1920s and 30s.

Both components, collar and necktie, are backed with cotton cloth and edged with a decorative beaded edging technique. Two separate variants of blue are employed in the background. This was a common occurrence in Native American beadwork, when bead supplies dried up and new stocks of beads were of a different batch and the color match was imperfect.

From the 1920s, the collar and necktie was adopted as a new fashion accessory by Northern grass dancers. These versions were often made of dark fabric and decorated with colored sequins, rick-rack braid, and commercial fringe. They were popular for several decades among the Blackfoot, Stoney, Sarsi, Plains Cree and Plains Ojibwa.

As Canadian Plains beadworkers always had to be on the lookout for viable ideas to supplement their incomes on the reserves, some sets were made for sale to early tourist visitors to the Rocky Mountains area.

The vogue for collar and necktie sets did not fade out completely after the 1930s. Collar and tie sets continue to be made and worn with traditional outfits by the modern-day Blackfoot and Stoneys, particularly for parades and other ceremonial events. They were worn in conjunction with either beaded buckskin shirt or fully-beaded vest.

The Warrior's World
Dance Regalia

ARAPAHOE INDIANS AT FRONTIER DAYS, (POWBLEARY)

Roach, Northern Plains, Blood Blackfoot, circa 1920

Porcupine guard hair, deer hair, horsehair, woolen yarn, cotton thread, glass button. Length (base) 35.5 cm

The roach headdress of porcupine guard hair and deer hair is an important style of headgear which originated among eastern tribes and became popular with many Plains tribes in the nineteenth century. In early times, its use related to specific Pawnee warrior societies, though it was eventually adopted as part of 'Omaha Dance' regalia which was passed from the Pawnees via the Omaha and Osage to other Plains groups. Among certain groups, turkey beard was an alternative choice of material for roach construction.

This roach, collected from the Blood Reserve in southern Alberta in the 1920s, has a base of plaited wool and horsehair. The porcupine guard hair is trimmed, to both outside and inside, with rows of orange-dyed deer hair.

Roach, Central Plains, Teton Sioux, Pine Ridge Reservation, circa 1970

Porcupine guard hair, deer hair, woolen yarn, linen thread
Length (base) 51 cm

The 'porky' roach is today worn as part of Pan-Indian male pow wow regalia—by traditional dancers, grass dancers, fancy dancers, and chicken dancers. The extreme length of the base is a relatively recent development, particularly popular among modern fancy dancers. This roach was purchased by the author from an Oglala Sioux friend, formerly a fancy dancer, on Pine Ridge Reservation, South Dakota, in the 1970s.

Roach feather, Central Plains, Teton Sioux, Pine Ridge Reservation, 1950s

Eagle feather, bone, copper wire
Length 34 cm

This eagle feather in a cylindrical bone socket was in use at Pine Ridge Reservation until the 1970s when it was given to the author by an Oglala Sioux friend. It attaches to the roach spreader by means of copper wire.

Dance ornament, probably Northern Plains, early twentieth century

Woolen cloth, sequins, glass beads, paste jewelry, cotton edging
Length 79 cm

Probably the trailer to a dance bustle, or possibly a grass dancer's back apron, this dance ornament is constructed of a rectangular piece of black woolen cloth, the lower end bifurcated. It is decorated overall with a geometric arrangement of sequins and tubular glass beads. Numerous rhinestone jewelry ornaments add to the effect.

Dance harness, Northern Plains, early twentieth century

Velvet, glass beads, wool, cardboard, commercial trimming, silk ribbon, cotton fabric
Length (maximum) 101.5 cm

This item of 'grass dance' regalia consists of two vertical bands of black velvet applied with eight beaded rosettes. To the center is a rectangular panel of couched overlay beadwork with stylized floral and geometric decoration and a wool yarn fringe below. It is further embellished with yellow silk ribbon and a variety of store-bought trimming, including metallic tinsel and brown tassels. The mixed media used in its construction illustrate the art of the Indian craftworker in selecting materials from the white man's world to create something innovative and very 'Indian' in taste.

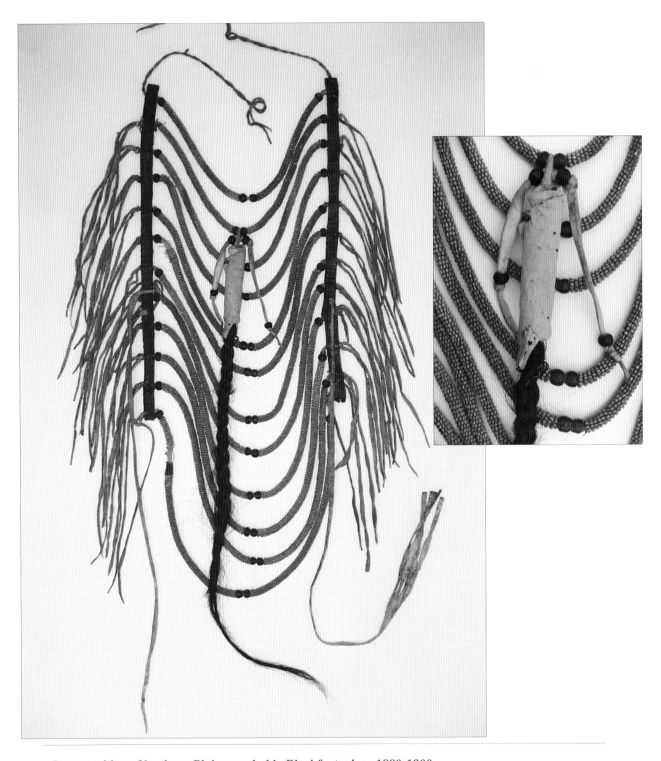

Loop necklace, Northern Plains, probably Blackfoot, circa 1880-1900

Glass and metal beads, harness leather, cotton cloth, buckskin, human hair, ermine skin, cotton thread
Length 50 cm

This style of necklace was much favored by the Blackfoot of both Alberta and Montana, as well as other Northern groups. It is constucted of twelve bead-wrapped cloth rolls of graduated length, strung between vertical strips of harness leather, with a buckskin fringe to each side. A long length of plaited human hair, wrapped in denuded ermine skin, hangs from the second beaded loop.

Belt set, Northern Plains, Stoney-Assiniboine or Plains Cree, circa 1885

Harness leather, brass tacks, native leather, glass beads, woolen cloth, metal
Length (belt) 92 cm, (pennant flap pouch, excluding tassels) 32 cm

This matching belt set comprises a large pennant flap pouch and pair of beaded and fringed strike-a-light pouches, all attached to a broad belt of heavy harness leather with domed brass tack decoration. It is uncertain whether such belt sets were used by men or women, as a few similar examples also include matching awl case and knife case as part of the ensemble.

Accessories of this kind exemplify the way in which a utilitarian article has evolved over time into an impressive and highly decorative piece of regalia, and epitomizes the fashion for heavy ornamentation in the late nineteenth and early twentieth century.

Together with a group of related Northern Plains items, the belt set was collected in the late 1880s by an engineer working on the Canadian National Railroad.

[Green, 2001 b]

Dance bustle, Central Plains, Teton Sioux, Pine Ridge Reservation, circa 1970

Eagle feathers, rawhide, silk ribbon, wood, metal, glass mirror, cotton cloth, linen tape
Length (overall) 148 cm

Feather bustles, known as 'Crow belts', were worn by members of military societies of the Pawnee, Ponca and Omaha. In the 1860s, the Teton Sioux adopted warrior society ceremonies and associated regalia from the Omaha, and formed what they called the 'Omaha Dance'.

Crow belts consisted of a circle of bird of prey feathers with hide or cloth trailers attached. Bird of prey feathers were associated with warfare due to the way in which these birds scavenged the battlefield after conflict. The two 'spike' feathers projecting from the top of the bustle represented two warriors killed in battle – one a friend, the other an enemy. To the belt were traditionally attached braided lengths of sweetgrass, which gave rise to the alternative term 'Grass Dance' for this style of outfit and the dances that accompanied it.

In the 1970s, an emerging style of dance outfit known as the 'traditional' style reflected elements of men's old-time dance regalia, including the eagle feather bustle. This dance bustle was a gift to the author from an Oglala Sioux friend on Pine Ridge Reservation, South Dakota, in the 1970s. It seems to have been refurbished from an older bustle.

Cuffs, Northern Plains, Stoney-Assiniboine or Blackfoot, 1890s
Glass and metal beads, canvas, cotton thread
Length (each) 32 cm, width 19 cm

This large pair of cuffs is almost certainly of Stoney origin. They are beaded in couched overlay technique on canvas. The hourglass designs with small projections to each end were much favored by the Stoneys. Note the smaller-scale motifs between the main hourglasses and to the periphery of the beaded field, composed of small rectangular blocks. The beaded design incorporates faceted brass beads. The right-hand cuff has lost its buckskin fringe. A similar pair of cuffs is worn by the Stoney man photographed on page 13.

Cuffs, Central Plains, probably Teton Sioux, circa 1930-40

Native leather, glass beads, woolen cloth, sinew, metal fasteners
Length (each) 13 cm

Male dancers wore either beaded, quilled or metal cuffs. This beaded pair dates from the late reservation period. Each side is decorated in lane-stitch with a different design. By the time these were made, old-time Venetian beads were being abandoned in favor of brighter Czech bead colors, which began to be available from around 1905. Many Sioux beadworkers continued to use sinew in their beadwork until fairly recent times. Beaded cuffs remain popular accessories for dance outfits, usually sewn with Nymo or cotton thread.

Armbands, Central Plains, Teton Sioux, Pine Ridge Reservation, circa 1940

Native leather, glass beads, sinew
Length 28.5, 27.4 cm

This pair of beaded armbands was a gift from Jack Red Cloud to Harry Cornish, a member of U.S. Air Force, while the airman stayed on Pine Ridge reservation in the 1930s or 40s. They are beaded in typical Sioux style in lane-stitch on thick brain-tanned hide. The outermost lanes of beadwork are slightly narrower than the inner lanes. The beads are of Czech origin, sinew-sewn.

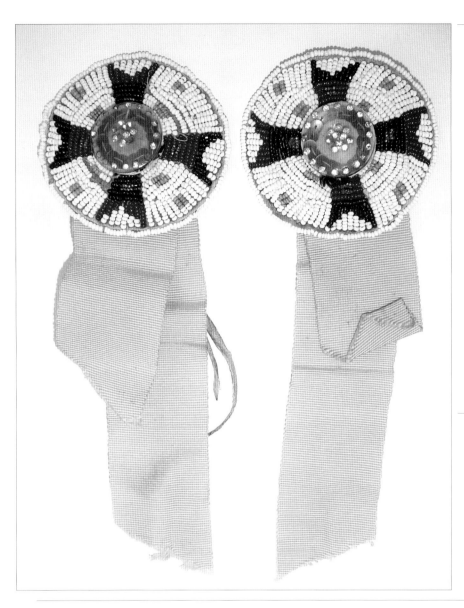

Rosettes, Central Plains, Teton Sioux, Pine Ridge Reservation, circa 1930-40

Native leather, glass and metal beads, rawhide, sinew, plastic, grosgrain ribbon
Diameter (each) 9 cm

These beaded rosettes formed part of an old style Sioux dance outfit from the 1930s, probably used on dance aprons. They are beaded on brain-tanned buckskin, with rawhide discs on the back and buckskin laces for attachment. At the center are early plastic buttons with sequin decoration. They were a gift to the author from an Oglala Sioux friend at Pine Ridge in the late 1970s or early 80s.

Dancer's leg bells, Central Plains, Teton Sioux, Pine Ridge Reservation, circa 1960

Steel, textile, leather
Length (each) 35 cm

Metal bells were popular trade goods on the Plains from times of early contact. Small brass 'hawk' bells were used to adorn a variety of ceremonial items and clothing. Larger sleigh bells were used by dancers from most Plains tribes. This set of leg bells was used for many years at Pine Ridge by a Sioux friend of the author's.

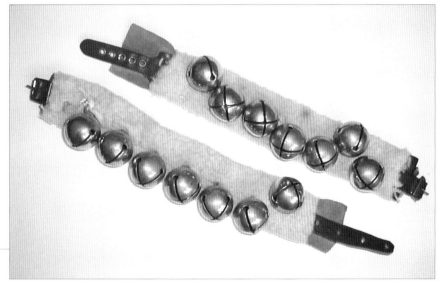

Ribbon shirt, Central Plains, Omaha, circa 1970

Synthetic textile, cotton, silk
Length 70 cm

Ribbon shirts became increasingly popular with 'traditional' dancers from the early 1970s onwards. This shirt, made of burgundy colored fabric, is decorated with yellow, green and orange silk ribbonwork. The cuffs are lined with a blue cotton fabric. It was made by an Omaha woman and belonged to an Oglala Sioux friend of the author's from Pine Ridge reservation, South Dakota, given to the author in the late 1970s.

Fan, Central Plains, Teton Sioux, Pine Ridge Reservation, circa 1910

Eagle wing, cotton fabric
Length 62 cm

Fans made from the entire primary section of an eagle's wing were carried by Plains male dancers, as well as being used for ritual purposes. The handle of this eagle wing fan is wrapped with a floral patterned cotton cloth. It was a gift to the author from an Oglala Sioux friend in the late 1970s.

The Woman's World
Tools and Implements

Pre-reservation nomadic camp life was harsh and demanding. Life for Plains women revolved around the keeping of the home and family. Women dismantled and erected the tipi when it was time to move camp, and prepared meat brought back from the hunt. They dried strips of meat in the sun to produce 'jerky', and pounded meat and chokecherries on stone slabs, mixing it with boiled fat to make 'pemmican'. These nutritious dried foodstuffs were stored in rawhide parfleche cases throughout the winter months. Other Plains peoples, such as the Mandan and Hidatsa, lived in earth lodges as well as tipis. Their women cultivated maize, squash, beans and other crops, supplementing food from the hunt.

In traditional Plains society, women were usually the owners of domestic tools and implements, tipi furniture, as well as certain items of horsegear. In some tribes, they formed sacred beadwork and quillwork guilds which regulated the production of domestic items, including cradles, tipi liners, pillows, and tipi bags.

In the reservation period, women were freed from the labors of their former nomadic lifestyle and had time to devote to the production of large quantities of beadwork. As well as for indigenous use, beadwork was made for trade and sale to supplement their generally meager incomes.

This young Brûlé Sioux girl is identified as Fanny Crazy Cat from Rosebud Reservation, South Dakota. She wears a splendid dress of woolen trade cloth with undyed selvedge, the yoke of which is decorated with dentalium shells. The simple design of rosettes to the hemline are also made up of dentalium shells; the crosses are executed in metal sequins. This form of decoration is a typical feature of this style of dress. (See chapter, *Something Splendid I Wear*). The girl's outfit is complemented with beaded leggings and moccasins, her pony equipped with a finely beaded saddle blanket and western saddle. The photograph, by an unknown photographer, dates circa 1910.

Written Heritage Collection

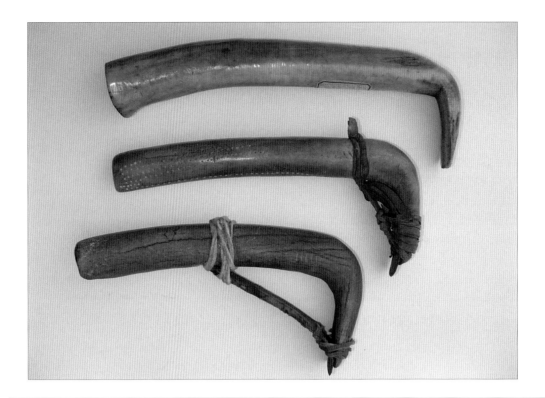

Hide scraper, Southern Plains, nineteenth century *(top)*
Elk antler
Length 34 cm

Hide scrapers with straight shafts were fashioned from the fibula of a deer or other large mammal. L-shaped examples, called *wahinkte* by the Sioux, were made from sections of elk antler by most Plains tribes from early times, and were used to de-flesh animal hides. This scraper probably dates back many generations. The end has been flattened to hold a metal blade, now missing. The handle end is pierced with a hole to accommodate a hide carrying thong which probably also served to increase the tool's leverage when in use. A series of faintly scored lines are without doubt the owner's record of the number hides fleshed.

Hide scraper, Plains, nineteenth century *(center)*
Elk antler, iron, leather
Length 29.5 cm

Made in characteristic L-shape, the end of this scraper has been flattened to hold a curved iron blade which is encased in dark-colored commercial leather, possibly recycled from a leather boot, and the blade held in position by means of buckskin thongs. There is an arrangement of incised dots and slashes, (some colored black), doubtless representing the number of hides tanned by the owner or owners. This is one of two hide scrapers that came from the Lola Lawrence collection, Oklahoma City.

Hide scraper, Southern Plains, nineteenth century *(bottom)*
Elk antler, iron, leather
Length 27 cm

This L-shaped elk antler hide scraper is a typical Southern Plains type, with iron blade, curved at the wide end and fixed in position at each end with hide thongs, spanning half the length of the antler handle. The blade is encased in smoked hide, sinew-stitched at each side. The top of the handle has a row of small incised dots and four incised slashes; the side incised with a further five slashes. This scraper also came from the Lola Lawrence collection, Oklahoma City.

Maul, Plains, mid-nineteenth century
Stone, wood, rawhide, textile
Length 20 cm

Mauls or 'berry mashers' of this type were used by all Plains tribes from early times for a wide range of purposes including pounding dried meat or choke cherries and driving stakes. The shaped head with flattened pounding surface was held between a length of bent cherry wood, the whole head encased in wet rawhide, resulting in an extremely functional tool.

Ladle, Plains, circa 1880
Buffalo horn
Length 23.5 cm

Spoons, dippers and ladles were made by Plains tribes from the horns of buffalo, bighorn sheep. Later examples were made from cow horn. The unworked horn was first softened in heated water and, when sufficiently pliable, shaped according to function. In the buffalo hunting days, domestic utensils, as with most items of tipi equipment and furniture, were the property of women.

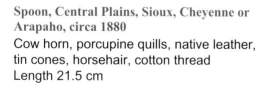

Spoon, Central Plains, Sioux, Cheyenne or Arapaho, circa 1880
Cow horn, porcupine quills, native leather, tin cones, horsehair, cotton thread
Length 21.5 cm

Spoons used for special occasions such as feasts were elaborately decorated with porcupine quillwork or beadwork. The handle of this finely shaped spoon is wrapped with plaited quillwork. Attached to the end of the handle are four buckskin lace suspensions wrapped with red quills, terminating in red horsehair-filled tin cone jingles.

Awl case, Central Plains, possibly Teton Sioux, circa 1890 *(right)*
Native leather, glass beads, rawhide, calico, sinew, metal cones, horsehair
Length 19.5 cm

Bone or steel awls were probably the most important tool in a woman's sewing kit. They were kept in tapered cases, usually suspended from the owner's belt. This awl case has a rolled rawhide core, covered in calico and spirally wrapped with beads. The flap is beaded with lane-stitch beadwork. Tin cones and yellow dyed horsehair complete the decoration and made a pleasing sound when it was worn or in use.

Awl case, Central Plains, possibly Blackfeet, circa 1900 *(left)*
Glass beads, wood, calico, native leather
Length (excluding fringe) 27 cm

Some awl cases were more decorative than functional. Judging by the interior compartment, this example would accommodate only the finest of awls. The whittled wooden core is covered in calico and wound along its length with glass beads. It has a fitted domed cap, with beaded tab attached to the suspension thong.

The Woman's World
Tipi Furniture

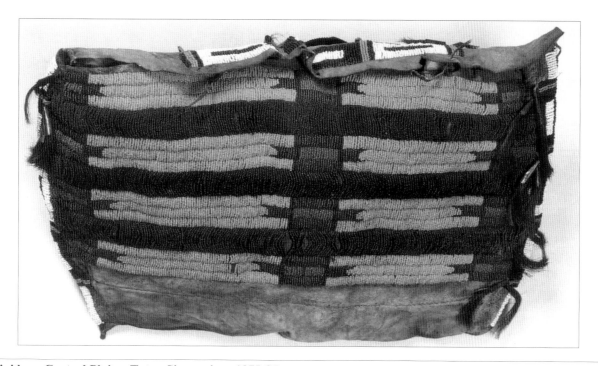

Tipi bag, Central Plains, Teton Sioux, circa 1875-85
Native leather, glass beads, tin cones, horsehair
Length 50 cm

Tipi bags, or 'possible bags' as they are called by the Sioux, were one of the most handsomely decorated of all tipi furnishings. They were made by the Sioux, Cheyenne Arapaho and various other Central Plains groups, usually in matching pairs, and were used for general storage purposes in the tipi, coupling as saddle bags in the days when the Plains Indian bands moved camp. A well equipped lodge might have several pairs, arranged against the perimeter of the tipi interior.

Early Sioux examples were traditionally decorated with narrow lines of dyed porcupine quills, usually red, running horizontally across the front field, often embellished at intervals with red-dyed fluffy feathers. This style of decoration, which persisted well into the twentieth century, was considered sacred. It was usually associated with craftwork guilds, and similar quilled lines were commonly applied to a range of women's belongings, including cradles, pillows, robes, moccasins and tipi liners, in addition to tipi bags.

The earliest surviving beaded examples, which date from the middle of the nineteenth century, are decorated with simple lane-stitch bands of glass 'pony beads', manufactured in the Venetian glass factories and acquired by Indians from traders.

Eventually, smaller 'seed' beads began to be available, firstly in limited quantities, and in a wider palette of Venetian colors. By the 1860s or 70s, with an increased availability of seed beads, tipi bags with heavily beaded fronts became fashionable among the Sioux and neighboring tribes. With the passing of the old buffalo hunting days and the enforced adoption of a sedentary lifestyle on reservations, the trend among the Sioux and their allies was for large expanses of lane-stitch beadwork in the adornment of ceremonial and everyday objects.

Parfleche, Intermontane, Crow, circa 1900
Elk? rawhide, paint, native leather
Length 75 cm, width 34.5 cm

Large rectangular rawhide envelopes of this kind were commonly used throughout the Plains and Plateau regions. Derived from the French *pare une flêche*, meaning 'deflects arrows', the word describes the hard, semi-tanned hide from which the container was made, and from which shields were also constructed. The outer flaps were usually painted with bold geometric designs in either earth pigments or trade paints. Often made in matching pairs, parfleches could be used to hold a variety of personal requisites and clothing, as well as supplies of dried meat. Rawhide cases of other shapes contained medicine bundles and ceremonial equipment such as headdresses.

Rawhide flat case, Central Plains, possibly Teton Sioux, circa 1920
Rawhide, paint, glass beads, native leather, sinew
Length 31.5 cm, width 27 cm

Rectangular flat cases had a variety of uses—often to hold a woman's tool kit, including hide scraper or fleshing tools. This example, with painted design of paired hourglasses, was collected by John C. Hellson from the Blood-Blackfoot of southern Alberta, although may originate from one of the Sioux groups further south.

[cf. Torrence, 1994]

The Woman's World
Clothing

Woman's dress,
Central Plains, Teton
Sioux, circa 1915-25

Photo by David B. Bailey

So many people are under the impression that we disappeared with the buffalo or still live in tipis. It's good to let people know that our culture evolves. In fact, it's the ability to evolve and adapt that has kept us here this long. Our spiritual ways changed with the way our lives changed over time. Our prophets tell us that, as long as we can keep our language and ways alive, the Tsistsistas [Cheyennes] will walk the earth. So even though our lifeways may not seem as romantic as they were 150 years ago, we are still here, carrying on!

- Nico Strange Owl, Northern Cheyenne (March 2004)

Woman's dress, Central Plains, Teton Sioux, circa 1915-25 (opposite page)
Native leather, glass beads, sinew
Length 138 cm, width (excluding fringe) 174 cm

The earliest fully-beaded yoke dresses made by the Sioux were of tripartite (three-skin) construction and had yokes with simple geometric designs in lane-stitch beadwork on an open expanse of sky blue background, within linear striped borders. The skirt section was traditionally stained with yellow earth pigment. This style was the culmination of an increased availability of imported seed beads in the mid-nineteenth century.

Both the blue-beaded yoke and yellow-stained skirt were formalized conventions which have a parallel in men's ceremonial *wicasa* shirts, and appear to have their origins in the Sioux view of the universe. The yellow staining to the skirt represented *Inyan*, the Stone, the first element of creation. The blue yoke symbolized *Taku Skan Skan*, the 'Power that Moves', the Sky. The border of colored stripes represented *Wignunke*, the Rainbow, which arcs between Sky and Rock.

Another formalized convention was a distinctive U-shaped device positioned at the center of the breast. Although probably derived from the shape of the animal's tail on earlier two-skin dresses, this feature came to represent the Turtle, the creature associated with women's capacity for childbirth and the natural cycles relating to womanhood.

Later Sioux dresses are characterized by an expanded beaded area to the yoke, which employs more complex arrangements of composite geometric designs. A wider range of yoke background colors also became fashionable, including white and various blues. Skirt sections were left natural creamy white rather than yellow-stained.

This dress, made of brain-tanned elk hide, has a deep yoke with white-outlined composite designs on a medium blue field. The white border and blue secondary band below it contain alternating geometric composites. The turtle device is omitted.

In wearing such a garment, a Sioux woman symbolically places herself at the center of the whole universe, metaphorically creating the world anew from the center, assuming her place in the Creation. In doing so, she underlines the inseparability of the sacred and the profane in Sioux everyday life.

[Green, 1997 a ; Hail, 1980: 12 & 96]

Quapaw woman, Mu-Ska Tuhn-Ka, wearing Sioux dress with full beaded yoke. From a postcard published by Charles Banks Wilson, Miami, Oklahoma.

Written Heritage Collection

Woman's dress, Southern Plains, Cheyenne, circa 1930

Native leather, glass beads, mescal beans, cotton thread, sinew
Length 118 cm, width, excluding fringe, 89 cm

In terms of construction and style of decoration, this tripartite dress, although of twentieth century date, differs little from nineteenth century Cheyenne examples. It is made of brain-tanned elk hide, decorated with bands of lane-stitch beadwork to the shoulders and at bust level, the designs consisting of simple rectangular blocks with small triangular appendages.

The beaded zigzag devices to the lower hemline, enclosing triangular areas stained with red earth pigment, as well as the method of separately attaching each individual fringe, are all classic Cheyenne features. The extension tabs added to sleeves, waistline and outer corners of the skirt are age-old references to the legs of the animals whose hides are used to make the dress.

Woman's dress, Plateau, Umatilla, circa 1920-40

Native leather, glass beads, cotton thread, sinew
Length 112 cm, width, excluding fringe, 94 cm

Plains style hide dresses of binary (two-skin) construction were worn by most Plateau groups from at least the early nineteenth century. Their yokes were lavishly ornamented with bands of lane-stitch beadwork, often in pony beads. The contours of the beadwork emphasized the 'deertail' outline resulting from hides being stitched along the shoulder seam of the dress and surplus hide being folded down as a decorative feature. The tail was often retained, with fur intact, at the center of the yoke.

This twentieth century dress was collected by Duane Alderman on the Umatilla Reservation near Pendleton, Oregon, and belonged to Auralia Shippentower. It is of modified two-skin construction, with a panel of hide added in across the shoulders. The yoke is decorated with bands of lane-stitch beadwork in sparkling French beads, popular among the Plateau groups in the 1920s and 30s. The diamond-shaped motif at the center of the yoke is a vestigial reference to the deer's tail traditionally used on binary dresses from the Plateau region.

Piegan Blackfeet
woman's dress,
circa 1940.

Woman's dress, Northern Plains, Piegan Blackfeet, circa 1940 *(opposite page & below)*

Native leather, canvas, glass beads, deer dewclaws, brass bells, cotton thread
Length 129 cm, width (including fringe) 102 cm

This elegantly understated dress was collected around 1970 by John C. Hellson from the Night Shoots family of Browning Reservation, Montana. It is constructed of brain-tanned buckskin, with a yoke section of heavy canvas, applied with wide lanes of lane-stitch beadwork. The beads used are of 'pony bead' size; red, dark blue and white in color.

Just below the beaded field, to the front of the dress (opposite), is a row of suspensions of large beads and deer dewclaws; to the back (below), suspensions of tile beads and brass bells. From the neckline hangs a long bead-wrapped pendant with a cluster of eagle plumes to the end.

Woman's leggings, Central Plains, Northern Arapaho, circa 1870
Native leather, glass beads, sinew, tin cones, pigment
Length (each) 45 cm

Finely beaded hide leggings were worn as an accompaniment to many Plains women's outfits. Central and Southern Plains examples were usually decorated with panels of lane-stitch beadwork with geometric designs. Women's leggings consisted of a cylinder of hide, often irregular in shape at the top in accordance with the natural shape of the hide. The upper edge of some examples has a cut fringe, but is otherwise left plain.

Simple geometric designs from the 'early seed bead period' were much favored by conservative beadworkers when making women's leggings, even later examples. The use of buffalo hide, yellow ochre pigment, the heavy use of tin cone jingles, as well as finely beaded decorative edgings, all indicate an early date for this pair, which came from the collection of F. Dennis Lessard in the 1960s. According to Kroeber [1902: 49], the tin cone jingles frightened away snakes or biting insects. The band of green bead along the lower edge of the leggings is a traditional characteristic of many Sioux and Northern Arapaho women's leggings, and doubtless held some symbolic meaning.

Woman's leggings, Central Plains, Northern Arapaho, circa 1890-10

Native leather, glass beads, sinew
Length (each) 34 cm

This pair of women's leggings is decorated with extremely small Venetian beads. This fact, together with the use of a translucent red rather than a white-heart red, suggests an Arapaho rather than Teton Sioux provenance. The extremely simple geometric composition reflects the conservative taste of the maker, perhaps underlining the traditional importance of this item of clothing among Plains women.

Woman's leggings, Northern Plains, Blackfoot, circa 1890 (inset)
Canvas, woolen cloth, glass beads, native leather, cotton thread
Width (each) 33 cm

In the second half of the nineteenth century, Northern Plains women commonly adopted materials other than hide for making beaded leggings. This pair is made of canvas reinforced with navy woolen cloth, the surface fully beaded with geometric designs made up of small rectangular blocks, using the couched overlay beadwork technique. They belonged to a Blood Blackfoot woman named The Only Handsome Woman, wife of Dog Child. She appears in the photograph below, wearing these leggings, circa 1890. She also wears a Sioux style dress, or dress yoke, and a broad panel belt with areas of beaded and brass tack decoration. Dog Child, or Duck Necklace, was a North West Mounted Police scout. He is pictured wearing a buffalo coat, brimmed hat with fluffy feather trim and, unusually, holds a Japanese Samurai sword.
Photograph by Trueman & Caple (National Archives of Canada, PA-195224).

Trueman and Caple, Photo, Vancouver,
N. W. M. Police Indian Scout, Dog Child and Squaw Blackfeet Indians Gleichen, Alb.

A Warrior I Have Been

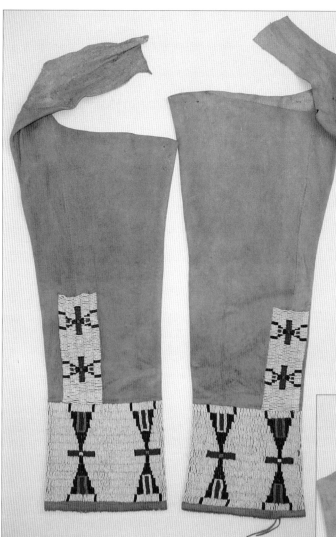

Woman's leggings, Southern Plains, Southern Cheyenne, circa 1900

Native leather, glass beads, sinew
Length (excluding tabs to top) 47, 51.5 cm, width (beaded panels) 15 cm

Made of finely smoke-tanned buckskin, this pair of leggings is decorated with panels of lane-stitch beadwork, thirteen lanes in depth. The designs are conservative in taste, typical of many Cheyenne and Arapaho women's leggings, consisting of paired hourglasses to both front and back. The leggings are sewn closed along their length. Fine buckskin laces to the lower edge serve to attach each legging to the wearer's moccasins.

Woman's leggings, Southern Plains, Southern Cheyenne, circa 1930

Native leather, glass beads, nickel buttons, cotton thread
Length (maximum) 55, 59 cm, width (beaded panels) 15 cm

The elongated form of this style of woman's legging allowed the upper edge to be folded over as a decorative feature when worn. The upper edge was sometime decorated with an integral cut fringe. This pair, acquired from a Cheyenne lady from Deer Creek community at Thomas, Oklahoma, features a conservative design of hourglasses, repeated three times on each legging. A row of nickel buttons is attached to the vertical side panels.

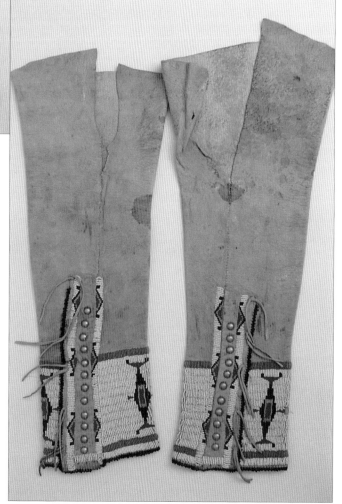

Woman's leggings, Central Plains, Teton Sioux, circa 1890-1910

Native leather, glass beads, sinew
Width (each, opened out) 45 cm

Teton Sioux women's leggings, particularly those made after 1880, tend to employ more complex arrangements of composite geometric designs in lane-stitch beadwork technique. Later nineteenth and early twentieth century examples were rarely made as closed cylinders but as large panels of beadwork which were wrapped around the lower part of the legs and closed by means of buckskin laces. This pair of leggings features split hourglasses with bifurcated appendages projecting from their narrowest point, divided by a secondary design resembling a vertebra. As well as old Venetian colors, the beadwork includes faceted steel beads, popular for several decades from the mid-1880s.

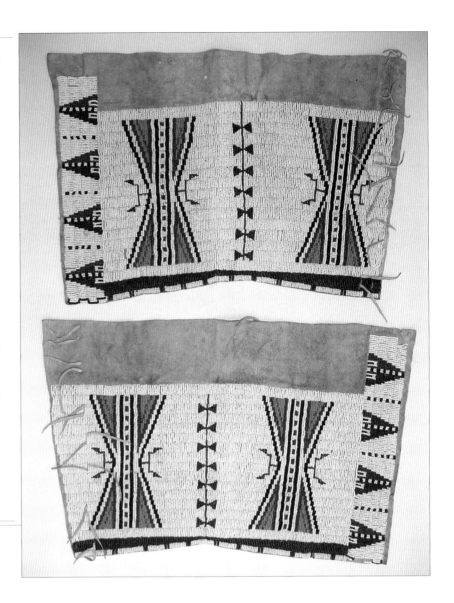

Belt, probably Plateau, circa 1875-85

Harness leather, glass beads, sinew
Length 88 cm

Both men and women from the Northern Plains, Intermontane and Plateau regions wore beaded panel belts of thick commercial harness leather with their traditional regalia. Sometimes beadwork was combined with areas of dome-headed brass tack decoration. This style of belt seems to have been quite widespread for many decades, although distinct tribal differences are difficult to determine.

Woman's belt, Intermontane, Crow, circa 1920-40

Canvas, glass beads, paper, cotton thread, native leather
Length 88.5 cm

Among Intermontane groups such as the Crow and the Shoshone, wide belts with finely beaded floral designs were popular from the early twentieth century onwards. Bold floral forms with lines tracing the veins on flowers and leaves, often executed in very small 'cut' beads, are typical of much beadwork produced in this area. This belt is beaded in extremely small seed beads on heavy duty canvas, reinforced with layers of thick brown paper.

Fan, Central Plains, Teton Sioux, Rosebud Reservation, 1970s

Feathers, leather, wood, glass beads
Length (maximum) 54 cm

Modern-day female traditional dancers usually carry a fan. This dance fan was purchased from a Brûlé fan maker by the author at Rosebud Fair, Rosebud Reservation, South Dakota in August 1979. It is constructed from a full set of twelve red-tailed hawk tail feathers, the quills of which are encased in a tapered hide sheath and set in a cylindrical gourd-stitch beaded handle.

Woman's purse, Central Plains, Teton Sioux, circa 1900

Native leather, glass beads, sinew, leather, metal, textile
Length 20.5 cm

This style of beaded clutch purse, decorated with lane-stitch beadwork on buckskin and applied over the framework of store-bought purses, was a popular fashion accessory used by Sioux women in the early years of the twentieth century. Larger items such as doctor's bags and violin cases were similarly decorated and were sometimes sold or given as gifts to non-Indians.

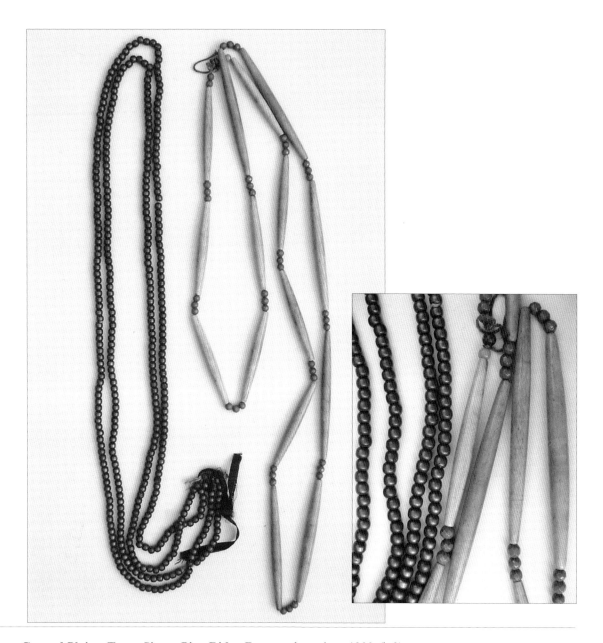

Necklace, Central Plains, Teton Sioux, Pine Ridge Reservation, circa 1900 *(left)*

Brass beads, string
Length 68 cm

This type of woman's necklace, made of old style hollow-ground French brass trade beads, was extremely popular among many Plains groups in the late nineteenth and early twentieth century. Bandoleers made of the same brass beads were worn by male old-time dancers. This necklace was a gift to the author from a Sioux friend on Pine Ridge Reservation in the late 1970s.

Necklace, Northern Plains, circa 1900-20 *(right)*

Bone hairpipes, glass beads, string
Length 94 cm

Made of bone hairpipes alternating with glass trade beads threaded on commercial string, this woman's necklace was collected by the Reverend A.W. MacMichael between 1914-20 while working as Head of the South Alberta Mission in Edmonton. In 1920, MacMichael returned to England to act as chaplain to the Archbishop of Canterbury.

Childhood

In the late nineteenth century, Plains Indian children were often dressed in miniature versions of adult clothing. The young Sioux girl in this charming studio portrait wears a woolen trade cloth dress, probably navy blue in color, the yoke section heavily decorated with dentalium shells and trimmed with ribbonwork. Her outfit is set off with beaded leggings and fully-beaded moccasins.

Written Heritage collection

Doll, Central Plains, Teton Sioux, circa 1920-40

Native leather, glass beads, wool, wadding
Length 38 cm

Simple cloth or buckskin dolls traditionally were made as playthings for Plains children. Many more, however, were made for sale for the curio market. While the majority tend to be dressed in female clothing, this beaded buckskin doll accurately represents in miniature the ceremonial clothing worn by Teton Sioux men – beaded shirt, leggings and fully-beaded moccasins. While nineteenth century dolls usually had human hair wigs, this example from the early twentieth century has braids of black woolen yarn.

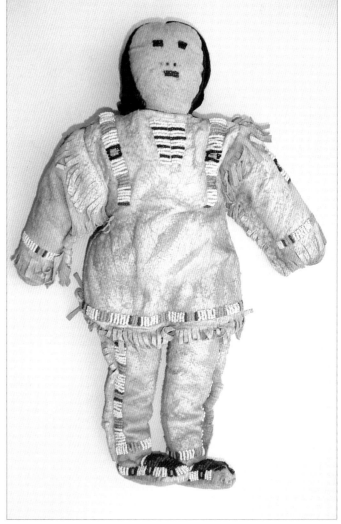

Navel amulet, Northern Plains, Blackfoot, circa 1880-1900

Native leather, glass and brass beads, cotton thread
Length (excluding suspensions) 15.8 cm

Used to hold a child's umbilical cord after birth, these containers were made by the Blackfoot either in the form of a snake (for a boy's cord) or a sand lizard (for a girl's). The Sioux made similar protective amulets, though probably not related to the child's gender. They were made in the form of lizards called horned toads, either quilled or beaded.

This example is fully beaded to each side, and the navel cord has been removed. This was a common occurrence when selling a navel amulet to curio collectors. The cord itself symbolized the sacred link between the mother and child.

Cradle cover, Southern or Central Plains, Cheyenne, circa 1885

Glass beads, canvas, rawhide, sinew, cotton fabric, native leather
Length 86 cm, width (at base of triangular cover) 61 cm

The soft cradle cover with triangular 'hood' was a versatile type of infant cradle particularly favored by the Cheyenne. Constructed of a triangular piece of native-tanned hide or canvas, reinforced with rawhide, they are decorated with lane-stitch beadwork, with wrappings of printed cotton or calico fabric. They are typically, though not exclusively, beaded with 'stripe' design of two alternating colors, most usually translucent dark green and white. It is popularly suggested that the stripes signify the 'life lines' of the infant - the paths of infancy, youth, maturity, middle age and old age.

The origins of the stripe, however, in early painted stripes deriving from war honors, and the subsequent quilled stripes applied in parallel rows to buffalo robes, pillows, tipi bags and tipi liners, underline the importance of this form of decoration in Cheyenne art.

The majority of Cheyenne cradle covers, whether of the stripe style or otherwise, feature a central rectangular unit which, when the cradle is in use, is positioned above the head of the child. This central unit may employ a simple counterchange theme or an entirely separate central design which interrupts the stripe design completely, dividing it into two distinct areas at either side of the central unit.

The use of red and yellow stripes on the central rectangular unit of this cradle cover may symbolize the life-giving powers of the sun and earth. Symbolic use of color and design is highly likely on Cheyenne articles relating to both childhood and womanhood. The rectangular tab above the triangular hood is a separate insert, projecting into the back of the cover and standing upright when the cradle is in use. The beaded decoration is applied directly onto the rawhide in wide bands of lane-stitch, creating a flat effect resembling overlay beadwork. Typical characteristics of the rawhide tab include square corner blocks, a central design (typically a cross, diamond(s), rectangle(s), or 'dragonfly' motif).

The wraps of patterned cotton fabric, lined with plain cream-colored calico, are typical of many examples of Cheyenne cradle covers. The infant was swaddled in a blanket and wrapped snugly in the cradle, with added padding to protect its head and, once in the cradle, could be carried or nursed in the arms, or left unattended in complete safety.

The Sioux made similar soft cradles with rectangular rather than triangular hoods.

[Green, 1990]

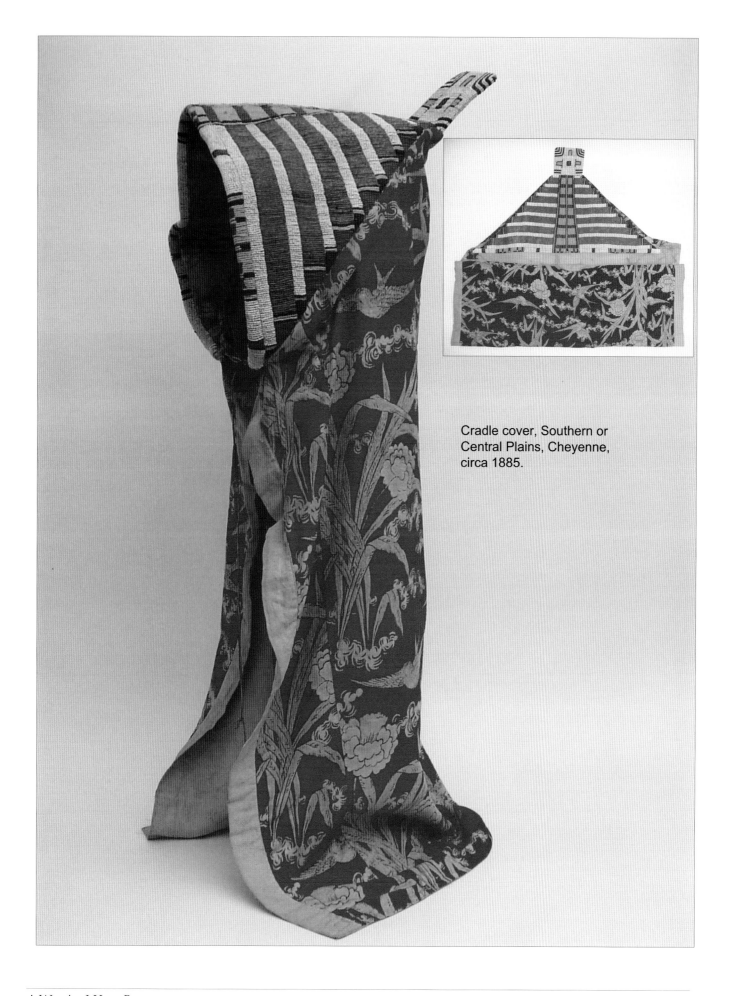

Cradle cover, Southern or
Central Plains, Cheyenne,
circa 1885.

Model cradle, Western Apache, circa 1890-1900

Model cradle, Western Apache, circa 1890-1900 (opposite page)

Native leather, glass beads, textile, wood
Length 21 cm

Miniatures and childhood-related items seem to have a universal appeal. This carefully made model cradle is of a type made the Western Apache groups of east-central Arizona. They are perfectly scaled-down and more highly embellished versions of the cradles traditionally used for child care by the Western Apaches. They may have been made for indigenous use as children's toys, as well as for sale to late nineteenth century and early twentieth century curio collectors.

The rigid framework is constructed of flat-section yucca wood slats fixed between a bent wood frame. Its most characteristic feature is the curved canopy or "shade" of buckskin-covered rawhide, lined with cream-colored cotton cloth. On full-size specimens, the curved canopy served as sun visor, wind-shield and, of course, protection for the infant's head.

The beadwork decoration features a range of traditional Western Apache designs, executed in lazy-stitch technique, commercial thread-sewn. A long bead fringe hangs from both the upper and lower edges of the canopy. The cradle is padded out with wrappings of floral-patterned cotton cloth, and may originally have contained a simple doll.

Late nineteenth century Western Apache beadwork is typically quite sparse and is usually applied to a range of buckskin articles in single lane-stitch lanes. These lanes are generally quite narrow, rarely wider than 1 cm, sometimes narrower, and consist of decorative borders and stand-alone motifs of protective or religious function, on a plain or yellow-pigmented buckskin ground. Borders often comprise repeated diagonal stripes, zigzag or sawtooth motifs, triangles, or longitudinal divisions of color.

Commonly used protective designs include arcs, crescents, and a variety of crosses and zigzags which seem to represent both "snakes" and "Lightning Power". For a discussion of these Snake / Lightning motifs in Western Apache iconography, see Ferg, 1987: 120-122. Another symbolic design is the combined cross and crescent, associated with the *daagodigha* religious cult of the early twentieth century. [Ferg, 1987: 133-5].

This model cradle is decorated with two main types of symbolic designs: crosses, and snakes / Lightning Power devices. Crosses are beaded to the front and top (both outside and inside) of the canopy, as well as to the main buckskin body, and the rectangular buckskin pillow. Flanking the crosses to the body of the cradle are two snake / Lightning Power motifs, with circular "heads".

Beads used on the model are size 5/0 Venetian, the colors being translucent amber, pale blue, translucent red, with some black.

In many respects, this model cradle represents a classic Western Apache object, exemplifying some of this group's most important stylistic and symbolic features.

Full size cradles of this type tend to be quite plain, the cover of buckskin, or more commonly canvas, often stained with yellow earth pigment, usually mixed with yucca juice as a binder. The curved canopy is generally constructed of flat yucca wood slats, these not usually being covered with buckskin or cloth, but left exposed.

The cover laces with buckskin ties, holding the infant securely in position, swaddled in cloth and crushed cedar bark. A hide strap allows the cradle to be carried or suspended, as required.

The Western Apache groups continue to make this style of cradle, the majority being made for sale for the Indian art market.

[Green, 2003]

Beaded ball, Central Plains, Teton Sioux, circa 1890-1910

Native leather, glass beads, sinew, cotton thread, cotton cloth
Diameter 7 cm

A ceremonial ball was used as part of a traditional Sioux ritual called the *Throwing of the Ball*. It was made of buffalo hide, stuffed with buffalo wool and painted red, the color of the world, with blue dots at the four quarters, representing the heavens, and two circles of blue paint encircling it, forming two paths connecting the four quarters. In uniting heaven and earth, it symbolized *Wakan Tanka,* or the Universe. [Brown, 1953: 132].

Model cradle, Southern or Central Plains, Cheyenne, circa 1880-1900

Native leather, glass beads, sinew, cotton fabric, ceramic
Length 10 cm

This charming toy cradle, possibly made for sale, is a miniature version of the traditional Cheyenne style of soft cradle cover, similar to the example illustrated on page 143. The triangular hood is made of thick brain-tanned hide, possibly buffalo, decorated with alternating stripes of light blue and red. The wraps of tartan patterned cloth contain a small porcelain doll.

Quilled and beaded balls were also made as children's playthings, sometimes suspended from the infant's cradle. In later times, they were made for sale to curio collectors and early tourists. The Sioux in particular responded to a demand for native curios and produced volumes of traditional style beadwork and quillwork for commercial sale. This material was often marketed via middle-men to stores in east coast cities.

This example is decorated with a central band of beadwork in 'salt and pepper' style, whereby mixed bead colors were randomly selected without regard to design. This was sometimes employed as a means of using up small quantities of beads. More often, however, it was a labor-saving technique for decorating articles made for commercial sale such as awl cases, knife sheaths and war club handles.

Horsegear

SADDLE BLANKETS

A prominent feature of this style of saddle blanket is the four fringed tab extensions, the precise significance of which is uncertain. They seem to have evolved from small decorated pendants which might have been a vestigial reference to whole animal hide saddle blankets popular among Plains groups in earlier times, with the legs retained. It seems possible that the extension tabs are symbolic representations of the animal's legs. [Green, 2002: 9]. Similar rectangular pendant panels were added as a decorative device to another form of Plains horsegear, the pad saddle, which was a common trade item among many Plains peoples in the early nineteenth century.

Brûlé Sioux saddle blanket, Rosebud Reservation, South Dakota, circa 1900.

Saddle blanket, Central Plains, Teton Sioux, Rosebud Reservation, South Dakota, circa 1900

Native leather, glass beads, canvas, sinew
Length (excluding fringe to tabs) 155 cm, width 72 cm, width of border 11.5 cm

This beaded saddle blanket originates from Rosebud Reservation, South Dakota, dating circa 1890-1910. It is pictured in an old photograph of two Brûlé Sioux girls on horseback, both astride classic seed-beaded saddle blankets. The photograph was taken by R.E. Royce around 1910.

The beaded borders are ten lane-stitch lanes in width, sinew-sewn on buckskin, edged and backed with canvas. The center panel is of cream-colored canvas, machine-stitched, and the entire blanket is canvas-backed. The blanket is trimmed with a white buckskin fringe, brass bells, red wool cloth, and fragmentary red and blue silk ribbon, to each of four extension tabs.

[Green, 2002]

Photograph by R.E. Royce, probably circa 1900-10, showing two Rosebud Sioux girls on horseback, both astride classic seed-beaded saddle blankets. The blanket used by the girl on the left is illustrated on opposite page.

Photo courtesy of Bill Holm.

Saddle blanket, Central Plains, circa 1895

Native leather, glass and metal beads, sinew, silk ribbon
Length (excluding fringe to tabs) 146 cm; maximum width 68 cm

This seed-beaded saddle blanket has wide beaded borders made up of eleven lane-stitch lanes to the long sides and ten lanes to the short sides, sinew-sewn on buckskin. Two main composite geometric designs alternate on a white background. Note the slight curve to the right-hand edge, as well as the two pairs of slits to accommodate the girth straps. Brass bells, Czech 'basket' beads and silk ribbon to ends of tabs.

The mixture of Yanktonai and Assiniboine influences to the designs employed, together with the strong use of faceted brass and steel beads as part of the design, form the basis of a probable Fort Peck reservation attribution for this saddle blanket.

[Green, 2002]

Martingale, Northern Plains, probably Blackfoot, circa 1900-15

Woolen cloth, glass beads, canvas, wood, native leather, cotton thread
Length 94 cm, width 15 cm

This style of martingale, or horse chest ornament, was produced for parade use by the Blackfoot, Stoney and Sarsi. According to Ewers [1945], it was a type traditionally used by women. It is decorated with bold floral forms in couched overlay technique on red woolen stroud cloth. Many martingales of this type are not curved, but straight bands, constructed of red, navy blue or black woolen cloth. This one is backed with canvas and reinforced at each end by wooden dowels. Some examples are ornamented with suspensions of beads and brass bells or thimbles along the lower edge.

It was collected by the Reverend A.W. MacMichael between 1914-20 while working as Head of the South Alberta Mission in Edmonton. During this time, MacMichael amassed a substantial collection of Northern Plains objects. He later returned to England to act as chaplain to the Archbishop of Canterbury.

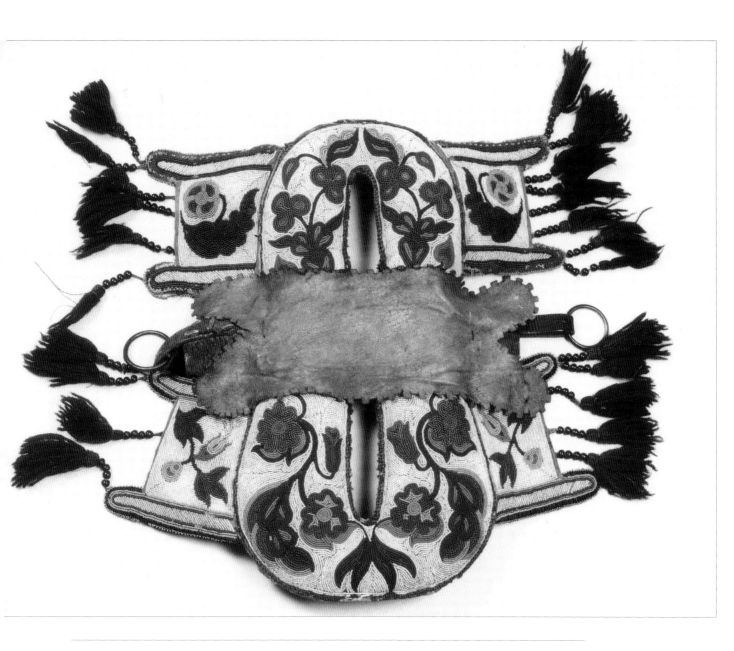

Pad saddle, Northern Plains, circa 1880

Native leather, canvas, glass beads, sinew, woolen yarn, harness leather, iron
Length 47 cm

Pad saddles were used by various Plains groups throughout the nineteenth century, and were a popular trade item. Used by younger men, early examples were fairly plain, rectangular, with simple quilled decoration in the form of roundels, diamonds and floral designs to the corners. They were usually padded with buffalo wool. The four decorated rectangular tabs attached to the sides may have represented an animal's legs – either those of the horse upon which the saddle was used; of the hide used to make the saddle itself; or indeed the saddle blanket, which was originally a complete animal skin with fur intact.

This pad saddle is highly embellished with floral designs in couched overlay beadwork.

Tobacco Bags

Among the tribes of the Plains the smoking of tobacco, known by the Sioux as kinnikinick, accompanied every ceremony. The pipe was a vehicle for prayer, the tobacco an offering to the Creator. Many groups obtained a reddish stone called 'catlinite' through trade from quarries in Minnesota. It was soft and easily carved, and was fashioned into pipe bowls of various shapes and sizes.

Pipes were often carried, together with tobacco and other smoking accessories, in specially made tobacco bags. The Sioux called these bags *cante ojuha*, or 'heart bags'. They were generally decorated with beadwork or porcupine quillwork, often with a decorative panel of quill-wrapped rawhide slats below the main decorated field. Different designs were used on front and back.

The earliest tobacco bags were probably made of entire animal skins, with porcupine quilled decoration. Pony-beaded examples were made in the nineteenth century until the availability of seed beads increased in the late 1850s or early 1860s. Generally speaking, the first seed-beaded Central Plains tobacco bags are long and narrow, with small panels of beadwork. Designs were executed in lane-stitch and often held symbolic meaning to the owner. Later examples were more ornate, with much larger panels of complex composite geometric designs, often more decorative than symbolic.

Northern Plains tobacco bags tend to be shorter in length than Central Plains examples, and usually lack the panel of quilled rawhide slats. They are beaded in couched overlay technique, usually with a different design to front and back, although some examples have a plain, undecorated back. The sides of the beaded panel often have a beaded rolled edge. The opening to the top of the bag is generally scalloped.

Sioux man holding a beaded pipebag with quilled panel. Photographed at Cheyenne Frontier Days, 1920s, by Jean and Marjorie Walker.

Written Heritage Collection

Tobacco bag, Central or Southern Plains, Cheyenne, circa 1880

Native leather, glass beads, sinew, pigment
Overall length 37 cm

Cheyenne tobacco bags were often of diminutive size, decorated with alternating stripe designs. This example, however, has an understated triangle design repeated to each side, the triangle surmounted by a T-shaped device. The line of transparent dark green underlining the lower edge of the beaded field, as well as the bead color palette of transparent dark green, cranberry red, corn yellow and light blue on a white ground, are typical Cheyenne characteristics. The body of the bag is rubbed with a red earth pigment.

Pipe, Plains, late 19th century

Catlinite, ash wood
Length 41 cm

This smoking pipe with T-shaped catlinite bowl and plain ash stem is probably an everyday pipe, possibly owned by a woman. Ceremonial pipes tended to be much more ornately decorated.

Reverse shown on facing page.

Tobacco bag, Central Plains, Yanktonai Sioux, circa 1870 *(extreme left)*

Native leather, glass beads, sinew, rawhide, dyed porcupine quills
Overall length 97 cm

This extremely long, skinny tobacco bag of brain-tanned buckskin has a small rectangular panel, sinew-sewn in lane-stitch. The simple hourglass and concentric rectangle designs on a sky blue background, the quillwork panel which flares out slightly to the base, as well as the finely cut fringe of equal or greater length than the bag itself, are all classic Yanktonai characteristics. This style of beadwork was popular around Devil's Lake, North Dakota.

Tobacco bag, Central Plains, circa 1880 *(second from left)*

Native leather, glass beads, porcupine quills, rawhide, cotton thread, pigment
Overall length 84 cm

The body of this elongated tobacco bag is stained with yellow earth pigment. The hide may be antelope. The beaded field, eleven lane-stitch lanes in depth, comprises a design of bars and rectangles in pastel bead colors, on a white ground. The panel of quilled rawhide slats below the beaded field is decorated with two elongated rectangles on an orange ground. The fringe, below, is also stained with yellow ochre pigment.

This example may originate from the Hunkpapa Sioux.

Tobacco bag, Central Plains, northern Teton Sioux, circa 1880 *(third from left)*

Native leather, glass beads, dyed porcupine quills, rawhide, sinew
Overall length 89 cm

The narrow, elongated proportions of this bag indicate a date somewhere in the 1880s. The lane-stitch lanes are very narrow, the beads a size 5/0 Venetian. The arrangement of square blocks to one side of the beaded panel probably represents the cardinal directions.

Judging by the designs composed of small rectangular blocks, as well as the range of bead colors used, it was probably made by one of the northern Teton Sioux groups, possibly the Minneconjou or Hunkpapa.

Below the beaded field is a panel of quilled slats with a design of four square blocks on an orange ground. At the base of the slats, threaded on the buckskin fringe, are dark blue Russian glass trade beads.

Tobacco bag, Central Plains, Teton Sioux, circa 1880 *(extreme right)*

Native leather, glass beads, porcupine quills, rawhide, sinew, pigment
Overall length 86.5 cm

The body of this tobacco bag has been liberally rubbed with yellow earth pigment. The shallow beaded panel, flaring slightly to the base, is decorated with paired hourglasses to one side, an arrangement of four rectangular blocks to the other. Both of these designs were commonly used on pre-1890 Sioux tobacco bags. The heavy buckskin fringe is also stained with yellow earth pigment.

Reverse shown on facing page.

Tobacco bag, Central Plains, possibly Teton Sioux, circa 1890-1900 *(left)*

Native leather, glass beads, dyed porcupine quills, rawhide, sinew
Overall length 67 cm

Although of basically Teton Sioux taste, this tobacco bag may have been made by another group. The dominant central composite unit to one side of the bag, flanked by smaller-scale elements in each corner, may indicate Arapaho influence. The Utes traded tobacco bags from the Sioux, and probably made many more themselves in Sioux taste.

The short quilled rawhide slats, as well as the lane of lane-stitch beadwork to the opening, are atypical of Sioux work.

Tobacco bag, Central Plains, Teton Sioux, circa 1885 *(center)*

Native leather, glass beads, porcupine quills, rawhide, metal cones, horsehair, sinew, pigment
Overall length 84 cm

The beaded panel of this tobacco bag consists of sixteen lane-stitch lanes, sinew-sewn. The split hourglass design to the front, with mirrored *tipi and clouds* motifs at center, is typical of late nineteenth century examples. By the mid-1880s, designs started to become more complex and composite in form.

The area within the triangular embellishments, above the main beaded field, are stained with green earth pigment. The small appendages, directly above these, are decorated with red-dyed horsehair-filled tin cones.

This bag was formerly in the collections of the Denver Art Museum.

Tobacco bag, Central Plains, Sioux, circa 1920-30 *(right)*

Native leather, glass beads, sinew
Overall length 71 cm

This tobacco bag, with its large beaded panel, twenty-two lane-stitch lanes in depth, dates from the period following the First World War, although the triangular tabs are a feature of some tobacco bags from an earlier generation. The complex arrangement of geometric designs, including chevrons and diamonds within a rectangular 'frame', as well as the use of some Czech bead colors, confirm a twentieth century date for this piece.

Reverse shown on facing page.

A Warrior I Have Been

Tobacco bag, Northern Plains, Blood-Blackfoot, circa 1880 *(center)*

Native leather, glass beads, sinew, pigment
Overall length 84 cm

The stylized semi-floral designs decorating the beaded field of this tobacco bag are typical of work from the Northern Plains region. The beadwork technique is couched overlay. Some of the beads are a tiny 'cut' Venetian type. The upper portion of the bag, as well as the inside, is stained with a red earth pigment. The triple-scalloped opening and shaped buckskin tab suspensions are common features of Blackfoot tobacco bags.

Tobacco bag, Northern Plains, probably Stoney-Assiniboine, circa 1880 *(right)*

Native leather, glass beads, sinew, pigment
Overall length 69 cm

The front only of this Northern Plains tobacco bag is decorated. The composition of stacked triangles, with borders composed of small square blocks, typify much Stoney beadwork from the late nineteenth and early twentieth century. The upper portion of the bag is lightly rubbed with red earth pigment. The scallops or 'ears' to the opening are common to many Canadian Plains tobacco bags.

Tobacco bag, Northern Plains, Gros Ventre, circa 1880 *(left)*

Native leather, glass beads, sinew
Overall length 68 cm

This tobacco bag probably originates from Fort Belknap reservation, Montana. The design to the front features a central diamond, the outer border composed of small square blocks. To the tip of each point of the diamond is a small cross, also built up of square blocks. The beadwork technique is couched overlay, the background color greasy yellow. The geometric units to the reverse side are beaded onto the hide first and the crow pink background filled in afterwards. The beaded panel is probably buffalo hide, the thinner hide to the body of the bag possibly antelope.

Reverse shown on facing page.

Tobacco bag, probably Canadian Plains or marginal Plains, circa 1880 *(left)*
Native leather, glass beads, dyed horsehair, sinew
Overall length 67 cm

This tobacco bag of lightly smoked hide is decorated to both sides with a complex floral composition of finely worked couched overlay beadwork within a simple linear frame. The top of the fringe below the beaded field is wrapped with dyed horsehair. Floral designs spread to the Canadian Plains groups from the tribes around the western Great Lakes region in the nineteenth century. Bags of this type were made by the Plains Cree, Plains Ojibwa and marginal Plains groups, and were popular trade items with the Canadian fur trading companies.

Tobacco bag, Canadian Plains, possibly Plains Cree, circa 1880-90 *(center)*

Native leather, glass beads, canvas, sinew
Overall length 77 cm

The floral-beaded panel of this Canadian Plains or marginal Plains tobacco bag incorporates a short inscription in the Cree or Ojibwa alphabet. The flower motif with four indented petals is a typically Cree feature.

Tobacco bag, probably Plains Ojibwa, circa 1880 *(right)*
Native leather, glass beads, sinew
Overall length 65 cm

The panel of this Canadian tobacco bag is decorated with finely worked floral couched overlay beadwork. The designs are complex and asymmetrical. One side incorporates the initials 'JH', probably either those of the owner or the maker. Unusually, the sides of the upper portion of the bag are fringed.

Bags and Pouches

Tobacco Canteen, Southwestern Plains, Ute, circa 1860

Glass beads, native leather, rawhide, metal, wood
Length 12.3 cm

This unusual combined tobacco canteen and necklace was made in the mid-nineteenth century by one the Ute groups of the southwestern Plains region. Such flasks are quite unique to the Utes, with the possible exception of the Jicarilla Apache.

The Utes are a Shoshonean people inhabiting central western Colorado and central eastern Utah. In the nineteenth century, the Utes were influenced by both Great Basin and Plains cultures, combining hunting and gathering with buffalo hunting.

Beaded tobacco flasks of this type seem to have been copied from silver tobacco canteens made around the same period by the Navaho Indians, neighbors to the south of Ute territory. Navaho silver versions were doubtless inspired by silver (and sometimes copper) tobacco canteens used by wealthy Spanish New Mexicans. Plain rawhide versions were apparently used by less affluent Spanish in New Mexico. The Utes, ideally positioned to take advantage of trading opportunities with both the Navahos and the Spanish, must have acquired both metal and rawhide tobacco canteens from an early date, and began making their own beaded versions by at least 1860.

The canteen is of flat, circular form with a cylindrical neck. The front is of buffalo hide and is fully beaded with concentric lanes of sinew-sewn lane stitch beadwork. The simple border design comprises four inward-facing triangles of translucent navy blue beads, each triangle surmounted by a T-shaped finial, on a white background. These devices are worked out in three concentric lane stitch lanes, the center in-filled with concentric rings of navy blue and white beads in couched overlay technique. Beads used for the main area of beadwork are Venetian, size 6/0.

This basic combination of dark design elements on a white ground is typical of the earliest seed beadwork produced by the Utes. The simple designs create a silhouetted effect, devoid of internal elaboration.

The back is constructed of thick buffalo rawhide, virtually black in color, with a glossy, crackled patination. The front and back sections are stitched together by means of sinew. The neck of the bottle is wrapped with size 5/0 Venetian beads in bands of navy blue and white, again sinew-sewn. The small circular stopper is fashioned of wood, and capped with a thick buffalo rawhide disc, the top of which is decorated with a simple incised circle.

Attached to one side of the flask, at two points, is a necklace consisting of large glass trade beads, threaded on a buffalo hide thong. The colors of the necklace beads are opaque white, translucent dark blue, black, and a single translucent green. The majority of the beads are spherical, of Venetian type; a few are cylindrical or ovoid in shape. One section of the necklace consists of a double-strand of buffalo hide lace, twisted, to which is attached a short length of brass chain, possibly of U.S. Army origin.

The canteen would have been worn around the neck as a necklace, with the flask hanging down upon the chest.

[Christie's, 1995: lot 79; Wooley, 1990: 97, fig.37; Wroth, 2000: 159]

Photo above:
Chippin, or Always Riding, a northern Ute, photographed in Washington DC in 1868. He is wearing a beaded tobacco canteen with geometric designs, similar to the one illustrated. This photograph, by A. Zeno Shindler, is one of the only known images of a Ute tobacco canteen in use.

Smithsonian Institution, National Anthropological Archives, 1489.

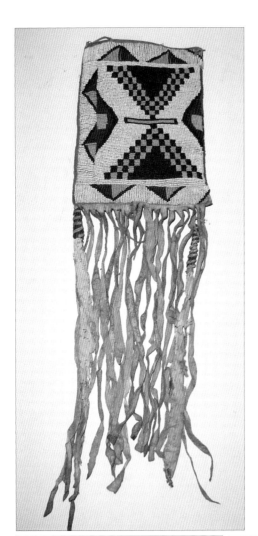

Mirror bag, Northern Plains, Blackfoot, circa 1880

Native leather, glass beads, sinew, woolen cloth, ermine skin
Length (maximum) 52 cm

This beaded mirror bag is decorated to front and back with geometric designs in couched overlay technique within lane-stitch borders. It appears to be have been recycled in Indian hands from the wide end of an old gun case or a woman's legging. This was common practice among Plains peoples, particularly during the early reservation period when resources were at a premium. The bag also seems to have had some kind of strap attached to the top, now missing.

Paint pouch, Central Plains, probably Arapaho, circa 1870
(front & back)

Native leather, glass beads, sinew, pigment
Length 21.5 cm

Made in the form of a tobacco bag, this paint pouch was used to hold earth paints. Judging by the red staining overall, it appears to have been used for vermilion. Miniature versions of ceremonial objects were often kept in bundles to symbolize the full-sized object.

Pouch, Northern Plains, probably Blackfoot, circa 1880

Native leather, glass beads, sinew
Length 11.5 cm

Small hide pouches were made for a variety of purposes, sometimes used to hold ceremonial objects and stored in medicine bundles. This pouch has a drawstring opening to the top. Each side is decorated with a different stylized semi-floral design. The hide is darkened with wear.
[Scriver, 1990: 182, 215 and 221]

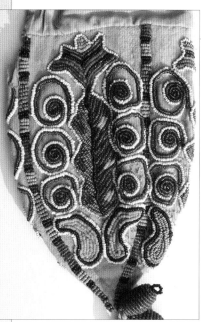

Tobacco pouch, Eastern Plains, Eastern Sioux, circa 1880

Native leather, glass beads, cotton cloth, porcupine quills, tin cones, dyed feathers, sinew, cotton thread
Length (overall) 41 cm

These three-sided tobacco pouches were based on the shape of an animal's scrotum, from which earlier examples were fashioned. This resulted in the popular name of 'scrotum pouch'. They were made by the Santee Dakota and Red River Métis of Minnesota in the nineteenth century, as well as certain mixed-blood Teton Sioux groups from South Dakota. The same distinctive semi-floral designs with white outlines are repeated on each of the three triangular buckskin panels, in a mixture of lazy-stitch and couched overlay beadwork, sinew-sewn, with vertical lane-stitch divisions.
[Green, 1989]

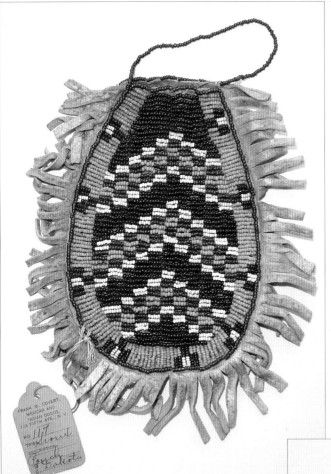

Pouch, Central Plains, Teton Sioux, circa 1890-1910

Native leather, glass beads, sinew
Length (including fringe) 18 cm

Oval pouches of this kind are generally described as women's pouches, possibly due to their shape which resembles the U-shaped 'turtle' device commonly seen at bust level on fully-beaded dress yokes. [Green, 1997 a: 12-17]. Large numbers of these were made for sale by the various Sioux groups, particularly the southern Teton Sioux, and were marketed via middle-men to dealers in the eastern states. This particular example has a retailer's tag attached, which reads *'FRANK M. COVERT, MEXICAN AND INDIAN GOODS, 329 FIFTH AVE., N.Y.'*

Pouch, Central Plains, Teton Sioux, circa 1915-30

Native leather, glass beads, sinew
Length, including fringe, 22.5 cm

This U-shaped drawstring pouch is made of very fine, smoked buckskin and is decorated with a border of lane-stitch beadwork incorporating repeated zigzag designs. The opening is cut with decorative 'swallowtail' tabs.

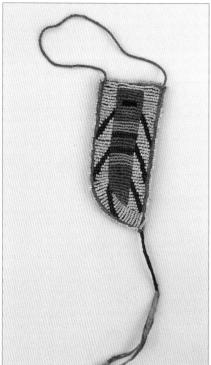

Knife case, Central Plains, probably Teton Sioux, circa 1875-1885 *(above)*

Native leather, rawhide, glass beads, sinew, paint
Length, excluding fringe. 22 cm

Judging by the painted designs to the rawhide back of this beaded knife case, it has been recycled from an old parfleche container. The front is decorated in lane-stitch beadwork with stepped-sided triangles. The cross-hatching to the back is characteristic of Hunkpapa work from Standing Rock, North Dakota. This attribution is borne out by the choice of designs and palette of colors used in the beadwork.

Knife case, Central Plains, Teton Sioux, circa 1900

Native leather, glass beads, porcupine quills, sinew
Length. excluding quilled suspension, 10 cm

Miniature versions of everyday objects were frequently made as children's playthings, and miniature ceremonial objects sometimes stored in medicine bundles to represent the full-sized article. This small beaded knife case may have been made for a child, or for the curio market. Some of the beads are of the tiny, 'cut' type.

Pouch, Intermontane, Crow, circa 1900-10

Native leather, glass beads, sinew
Length 19 cm

This gold poke pouch is decorated with simple horizontal bands with small triangular appendages. Probably made for sale, it has a drawstring opening and serrated welt.

Pouch, Central Plains, circa 1870-80

Native leather, glass beads, sinew
Length, excluding suspensions, 8 cm

Although part of the A.W. MacMichael Collection which comprised almost exclusively Northern Plains material, this small strike-a-light pouch appears to be of Central Plains origin. It may be of Arapaho or Ute manufacture. Small rectangular cases of this type were commonly worn on the belt and were useful for holding fire-making equipment such as flint and steel.

Pouch, Northern Plains, Assiniboine, 1860s *(left)*

Native leather, glass beads,
Length (maximum) 24.5 cm

Small rectangular hide pouches had a variety of functions among Plains groups, being used, among other things, to hold flints and steel for fire-making, small mirrors, and ration tickets. The front of this pouch is beaded with a simple geometric design in couched overlay technique within a border of Crow stitch. There are traces of red pigment to the back.

Pouch, Northern Plains, Stoney-Assiniboine or Plains Cree, late 1880s *(right)*

Native leather, glass beads, sinew
Length (maximum) 25.5 cm

This strike-a-light pouch is part of a matching belt set collected in Alberta by an engineer working on the Canadian National Railroad in the 1880s, (see page 113). It is constructed of heavily smoked hide, the front surface beaded in couched overlay technique with a vertical arrangement of inter-connected diamonds, composed of small rectangular blocks.

Tobacco pouch, Northern Plains, Blackfoot, circa 1880-90

Native leather, glass beads, woolen cloth, cotton thread, ermine tail
Length 16.5 cm

This pouch, part of the A.W. MacMichael Collection, is decorated to both front and back with a panel of couched overlay beadwork in very small Venetian beads. Suspensions of Bohemian basket beads are attached to the sides. The designs are comparable with those on the Northern Plains vest on page 103.

Watch case, Northern Plains or Intermontane, circa 1890-1900 *(left)*

Native leather, glass beads, sinew, cotton thread
Diameter 8 cm

This finely beaded circular case was probably intended to hold a pocket watch. The front is decorated in couched overlay technique with a concentric design, sinew-threaded, commercial thread-couched. It may have been made for sale.

Watch case, Northern or Marginal Plains, circa 1880-1900 *(right)*

Native leather, glass and metal beads, cotton fabric, cotton thread
Diameter 9.5 cm

Constructed of lightly smoke-tanned hide, this watch case was probably made for sale to early curio collectors or tourists. The front is fully beaded in couched overlay technique with a floral rosette composed of alternating concentric bands of dark blue and translucent red, with a center of faceted brass beads, it is lined with check-patterned cotton cloth.

Pouch, Northern Plains or Canadian Subarctic, circa 1885-1900

Native leather, glass beads, cotton thread
Length 16.5 cm

This pouch may originate from one of the Canadian Plains groups who, in common with several of the Subarctic peoples further north, produced floral beadwork in this style. It may have been used to hold tobacco or small items of ceremonial or medicinal significance.

Charm pouch, Southern Plains, Kiowa, circa 1880-1900

Native leather, glass beads, cotton thread
Length 14 cm, diameter 8 cm

Exquisitely made using 'cut' seed beads, this circular pouch was probably used as a medicine bag to hold peyote. The cross device to the front, executed in couched overlay technique in extremely small beads, is typical of Kiowa semi-floral beadwork. The bright blue background is filled in following the contours of the central design. The pouch is further embellished with a heavy bead fringe and decorative beaded edging.

Beaded bag, Southwestern Plains, Apache, circa 1930 *(facing page)*

Native leather, glass beads, cotton thread
Maximum length 37 cm

This type of rectangular bag, with drawstring opening and heavy bead fringe, was popular from the turn of the century onwards among many Southern Plains tribes, particularly the Comanche, Kiowa and Kiowa-Apache in Oklahoma.

The style was probably influenced by the commercially available drawstring purses of the day, as well as the fashion for bead fringing on white women's clothing and accessories, and it quickly spread to the various Apache groups in neighboring Arizona and New Mexico.

The bag is constructed from a single rectangular piece of soft brain-tanned buckskin, folded at the middle, with seams stitched up the sides. The front is decorated in lazy-stitch technique with a large central diamond motif, fifteen lanes in depth, in white, bright blue, crow pink and transparent red beads, the stepped design outlined with a succession of small square or rectangular blocks. Each horizontal lazy-stitch lane is six beads in width, with a narrow gap left between each.

Flanking this central motif at opposing corners are four `Maltese' type crosses in transparent dark green outlined in white, one cross in each corner, the whole composition framed within a double lazy-stitch lane border. The inner border, just four beads in width, comprises simple alternating blocks of transparent dark green and white; the outer border, seven beads in width, has diagonal stripes of red, transparent yellow, bright blue and white. Note that the inner border forms a complete rectangular frame, while the outer border is used only on the sides and lower edge. The background is left unbeaded.

The central diamond motif with smaller appendages at opposing corners is a typical configuration for this style of bag. The combination of stand-alone motifs on an unbeaded buckskin ground, within narrow lazy-stitch lane borders, is a general feature of Apache beadwork. [Green, 2003].

Each fringe is threaded with beads, creating a striking effect of horizontal bands of color. From top to bottom these are: white, transparent dark green, white, bright turquoise blue, crow pink, bright turquoise blue, white, transparent dark green and white. Each separate bead fringe pierces the lower edge of the bag at the point where the buckskin is folded. Some examples have small loops at the end of the bead fringe. Others have a cut skin fringe.

The bag is decorated around the top opening and up each side with a modified "zipper" edging technique. Beads are a size 4/0 Venetian. All beadwork is commercial thread-sewn.

The reverse of the bag is undecorated, although many examples are in fact beaded on both sides, usually with different designs to front and back. On some examples, the skin is stained with a yellow earth pigment. In this case, it is a natural creamy white. Some examples of these ladies' bags are customized with metal or plastic clasps fitted to the opening.

The double drawstring is attached through small slits in the buckskin, spaced at intervals across the top of the bag.

Similar bags are still popular among Southern Plains women today, used as part of modern-day pow-wow regalia.

[Ferg, 1987: 100; color plate 15; Green, 2001 a: 16-17; Green, 2003: 26-29; Hail, 1980: 205, nos. 274-278]

Belt pouch, Intermontane, possibly Shoshone, circa 1920

Commercial leather, canvas, glass beads, native leather
Length 10.8 cm

U-shaped belt pouches were popular among the various Intermontane and Plateau groups from the late nineteenth century onwards, probably copied from leather bags and wallets used by non-Indians. The construction of this example is typical, with a fully-beaded canvas front flap concealing a pocket of commercial harness leather. It attaches to the broad panel belt by means of two loops on the back, the flap secured by means of buckskin laces.

Bold flowers and leaves with contrasting outlines and traced veins are typical of post-1900 beadwork from the Shoshone, Flathead, Crow and Plateau groups.

Belt pouch, Plateau, circa 1900-25

Cornhusk, woolen yarn, native leather
Width 10.3 cm

This rectangular belt pouch, made by one of the western Plateau groups, is constructed of woven cornhusk and decorated to front, back and inside with bold geometric designs in applied wool embroidery. Buckskin loops to the back serve as a means of attachment to the belt.

Moccasins

When the first white visitors arrived in the Plains region, the tribes they encountered wore moccasins made entirely in one piece, and decorated with porcupine quills.

Construction methods had changed by the mid-nineteenth century, and varied somewhat from one group to another. Moccasins with separate hard rawhide soles became the norm among many tribes, possibly influenced by the white man's shoe. With the increased availability of imported trade beads, they were eventually decorated with glass seed beads. From the early 1870s there was a fashion for fully-beaded moccasins in lane-stitch technique. Moccasins for everyday use tended to be rather more plain.

Further north, on the Canadian Plains, and in Montana, a side-seam construction was employed. Cut from a single piece of hide, with the exception of separate tongues and ankle extensions, these were stitched with sinew around the outer edge. Beadwork decoration was usually executed in couched overlay technique, although lane-stitch was also popular with some groups, probably influenced by peoples south of the Canadian border.

Moccasins, Central Plains, possibly Hidatsa, circa 1870

Native leather, rawhide, glass beads, sinew, pigment
Length 25 cm

These partially beaded moccasins may possibly originate from the Hidatsa, and are constructed of brain-tanned buffalo hide with rawhide soles. This style of beadwork decoration, consisting of a band of three lanes of lane-stitch, was produced by several Plains groups and seems to have been linked with traditional women's guilds. The upper third of the beaded design, just below the tongue, typically features stripes of contrasting colors. The lower two-thirds, in the case of this pair, has a saw-tooth design. The two sections are divided by a simple band of alternating colors. The area of hide at either side of the central panel is decorated with red-painted stripes, now barely visible. A closely related pair of moccasins was collected from the Hidatsa on Fort Berthold reservation between 1906-18 by Gilbert L. Wilson. [Taylor, 1991: 96, no.5]

Moccasins, Central Plains, possibly Arapaho, circa 1880

Native leather, rawhide, glass beads, sinew
Length 25.5 cm

This pair of moccasins may be of Arapaho manufacture. They are decorated with a simple T-shaped design in lane-stitch, a common layout for partially beaded moccasins in the nineteenth century. The central lane of beadwork is again divided in traditional fashion – the upper third in white-core rose, the lower two-thirds containing small square blocks of white-core rose on a white background. The soles are made of thick buffalo rawhide with a dark epidermis layer.

Moccasins, Central or Southern Plains, Cheyenne, circa 1880s

Native leather, rawhide, glass beads, sinew, canvas
Length 25.4 cm

Another variation of partially beaded moccasin design consists of a rectangular beaded panel enclosed within a perimeter lane of lane-stitch beadwork. This lane follows the seam around the outside of the moccasin, often terminating halfway along the inside of the foot. The rectangular panel is flanked with elongated triangular appendages. This pair has canvas ankle extensions.

Moccasins, Southern Plains, Southern Cheyenne, circa 1900

Native leather, rawhide, glass beads, sinew
Length 26 cm

These Southern Cheyenne moccasins feature a rectangular panel, five lane-stitch lanes in width, divided in traditional fashion. The upper third consists of alternating stripes of green and white; the lower two-thirds features 'Thunderbird' devices. The panel is flanked by small rectangular appendages, projecting at a slight angle. Formerly in the collections of Denver Art Museum, ex Drew Bax collection, this pair of moccasins was illustrated by Ty Stewart in his excellent article on Cheyenne moccasins. [Stewart, 1971: 5, P-D]

Moccasins, Central Plains, northern Teton Sioux, 1870s

Native leather, rawhide, glass beads, sinew
Length 24 cm

This pair of fully-beaded moccasins belonged to Yellow Horse, a chief in Sitting Bull's band of Hunkpapa Sioux who crossed the border into Canada following the Battle of the Little Big Horn in 1876. They were collected by a J. Loring around 1880 and were sent to his daughter in England in 1880.

In 1869, Yellow Horse was involved in a fight with Crows while hunting along the Yellowstone River and camped near the mouth of the Powder River. Under command of Sitting Bull during the winter of that year, Yellow Horse and seventeen others were wounded and thirteen killed. Thirty Crows were killed in the skirmish. [Vestal, 1957: 115]

The moccasins are finely beaded in lane-stitch technique, with buffalo rawhide soles and bifurcated beaded tongues. The paired triangular areas created by the central dividing lanes are sometimes referred to as 'buffalo tracks', for obvious reasons. The transverse lane of beadwork across the instep is a feature of older Sioux fully beaded moccasins, a detail the Sioux shared with their Cheyenne and Arapaho allies only until about the 1880s. Later Sioux moccasins, particularly those made by the southern Teton groups, generally lack this feature. Solid-color, stacked designs, as used in the perimeter lanes of these moccasins, are a further feature of earlier Sioux lane-stitch beadwork.

Moccasins, Central Plains, possibly Teton Sioux, circa 1880

Native leather, rawhide, glass beads, sinew
Length 19 cm

Constructed of heavily smoked hide, these fully-beaded moccasins have two perimeter lanes with two alternating designs—large triangles containing 'house'-shaped devices; and silhouetted hourglasses - both of which were preferences of the northern Teton groups as well as the Yankton and Yanktonai.

Moccasins, Central Plains, Teton Sioux, circa 1890

Native leather, rawhide, glass beads, sinew
Length 28 cm

The soles of this pair of fully-beaded moccasins are made of horse rawhide, the uppers with 'buffalo tracks' of juxtaposed dark blue and medium green beads, enclosing small rectangular blocks. The repeated triangular designs to the perimeter lanes are composed of small squares—a preference of the northern Teton groups. This pair may originate from the Hunkpapas of Standing Rock, North Dakota.

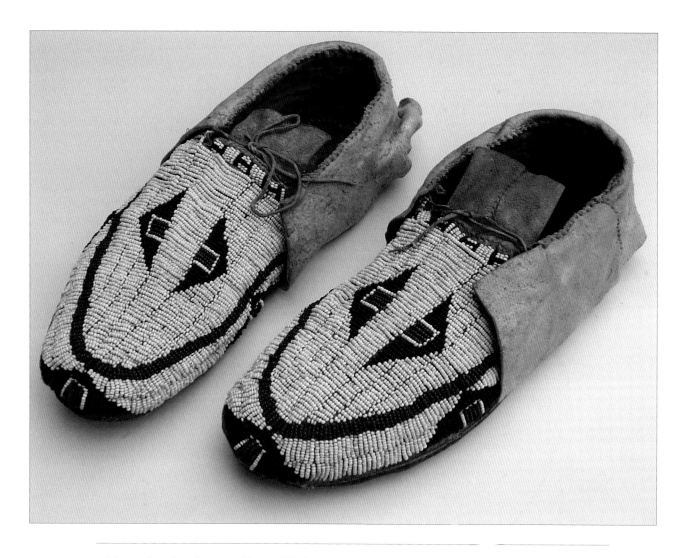

Moccasins, Southern or Central Plains, Arapaho, circa 1880

Native leather, rawhide, glass beads, sinew
Length 27 cm

The designs on this fully-beaded pair of moccasins feature arrangements of dark blue triangles and a narrow perimeter lane of white-core rose on a 'flooded' background of white beads. Large open areas of white were much favored by the Arapaho moccasin makers. Note the transverse lane of beadwork below the tongue—a feature of most fully beaded moccasins made by the Arapaho and the Cheyenne. The welt to the sole is probably indicative of a Southern Plains origin. This pair also has smoked buckskin ankle extensions.

Moccasins, Central Plains, Teton Sioux, circa 1890

Native leather, rawhide, glass beads, porcupine quills, sinew, canvas
Length 26 cm

The juxtaposition of beadwork and porcupine quillwork creates a striking effect. This was particularly popular among the Sioux and neighboring groups in the late nineteenth and early twentieth century. Quills were applied to the hide in the two-thread, one quill appliqué technique, sometimes called 'straight quilling'.

This pair of quilled and beaded moccasins was collected from the Cherrick family of Pine Ridge around the turn of the century. They are decorated with a V-shaped design on a red quilled ground within a border of two lane-stitch lanes.

Moccasins, Central Plains, Teton Sioux, circa 1900-11

Native leather, rawhide, glass and metal beads, porcupine quills, sinew, cotton fabric
Length 28 cm

A bright blue border of three lane-stitch lanes contrasts impressively with red quillwork infill on this pair of moccasins, which was collected in 1911 from Pine Ridge, South Dakota. The quilled design comprises a V-shaped arrangement of small triangles on a red ground. The beaded triangles to the border include faceted steel beads. The laces are quill-wrapped, the ankles edged with beige cotton cloth.

Moccasins, Central Plains, Teton Sioux, 1890s

Native leather, rawhide, glass beads, sinew, cotton fabric
Length 26.5 cm

This pair of moccasins has three perimeter lanes of lane-stitch beadwork and 'buffalo tracks' of medium green beads. Judging by the painted geometric designs to the inside of the soles, the rawhide from which they are made was probably recycled from an old parfleche container. The beaded tongues are trimmed with tin cones, the ankles edged with printed cotton fabric.

Moccasins, Central Plains, Teton Sioux, circa 1880

Native leather, rawhide, glass beads, sinew
Length 21.5 cm

This pair of youth's moccasins has a single perimeter lane of lane-stitch with repeated triangles and small square blocks. The 'buffalo tracks' of medium green beads contain diagonal arrangements of small rectangular blocks of red, blue and yellow. The transverse lane immediately below the tongue is a feature of pre-1890 Sioux moccasins, shared of course by the Cheyenne and Arapaho. The southern Teton groups, at least, seem to have abandoned this feature by the early twentieth century.

Moccasins, Central Plains, possibly Teton Sioux, circa 1880

Native leather, glass beads, sinew, cotton fabric, pigment
Length 26.5 cm

Although displaying generally Sioux characteristics, these fully beaded moccasins may in fact be of Ute origin. The soles are made of thick, crackled buffalo rawhide, the uppers of brain-tanned buffalo. The area of hide around the ankles is stained with yellow earth pigment. A narrow vertical lane of beadwork covers the heel seam. The ankles are edged with cotton cloth.

Moccasins, Central or Southern Plains, Arapaho or Cheyenne, circa 1880

Native leather, rawhide, glass beads, sinew
Length 22 cm

Around the 1890s, a new style of 'checkerboard' infill became popular among the Sioux, Cheyenne and Arapaho groups. It was also employed on small bags, and presumably enabled areas of beadwork to be covered more quickly.

These finely beaded moccasins are executed in extremely small Venetian beads, a fact which may indicate a southern, rather than a northern, Cheyenne or Arapaho provenance. An interesting constructional detail is that the tongues are integral and not separately added, a feature facilitated by the slanting cut of Cheyenne and Arapaho moccasins. The transverse lane of beadwork over the instep, as well as that running vertically up the heel seam, are all classic Cheyenne and Arapaho characteristics.

Moccasins, Central Plains, Sioux or Assiniboine, circa 1900

Native leather, glass and metal beads, sinew, velvet
Length 21.5 cm

'Honor' moccasins with fully-beaded soles were a development of the final decades of the nineteenth century and remained popular as a form of artistic expression well into the twentieth. They were made as special gifts to relatives, as well as for sale to curio collectors, and were regarded by the Sioux and certain neighbors as something of a status symbol. They were worn at dances and feasts by women from high ranking families, the beaded soles displayed to all with great pride.

This pair may originate from the Yanktonai or Assiniboine at Fort Peck, Montana. Incorporated in the colorful designs are faceted brass and steel beads, popular with the Sioux from about 1885.

Moccasins, Southern or Central Plains, Cheyenne, circa 1900

Native leather, rawhide, glass beads, sinew, silver
Length 23 cm

This colorful pair of fully-beaded moccasins is decorated with elaborate U-shaped devices in very small beads on a sky blue background. The perimeter lane has a repeated design of small triangles of white-core rose beads. On each tongue is stitched a domed concho fashioned from Morgan U.S. silver dollars.

Child's moccasins, Central Plains, possibly Teton Sioux, circa 1900

Native leather, rawhide, glass and metal beads, sinew, cotton fabric
Length 16.5 cm

These fully-beaded moccasins have three perimeter lanes of beadwork, the center lane of solid white-core rose. Red-outlined borders are commonly seen on fully-beaded moccasins from a variety of Plains groups. (See examples on pages 179 and 181.)

Child's moccasins, Southern Plains, Southern Cheyenne, circa 1920-40

Native leather, rawhide, glass beads, sinew
Length 18.5 cm

Judging by the shape of the rawhide sole and the bead colors employed, this pair of fully- beaded moccasins was probably produced by the Mohonk Lodge in Oklahoma in the 1920s or 30s. It is said that the arrowhead designs traditionally indicated an object was made for a boy. A range of different red beads is used, including an old Venetian white-core rose, a Czech opaque tomato red and a translucent red.

Child's moccasins, Central Plains, probably Teton Sioux, circa 1900

Native leather, rawhide, glass beads, sinew, cotton fabric
Length 15.7 cm

Symbolic designs were often used to decorate the uppers of part-beaded moccasins. This example bears a bold cross device, probably signifying the Four Directions, or the Morning Star. They were once part of the collection of Burton Thayer (1895-1979), president of the Minnesota Archaeological Society in the 1930s. Thayer collected actively from the 1920s to the 40s, mainly in the area around St Paul, Minnesota. His collection was dispersed in 1991.

Infant's moccasins, Central Plains, probably Teton Sioux, circa 1890 *(left)*
Native leather, rawhide, glass beads, sinew, cotton fabric
Length 11.5 cm

This tiny pair of fully-beaded moccasins illustrates the care lavished upon young children by their families. The Sioux regard children as a blessing from the Creator, and a pair of beaded moccasins was considered as an important gift to a newborn baby.

These moccasins have a perimeter lane of white beads with small colored blocks, and 'buffalo tracks' of translucent dark green beads. They also have high ankle extensions with a serrated edge.

Infant's moccasins, Central Plains, probably Teton Sioux, circa 1890-1910 *(right)*
Native leather, rawhide, glass beads, sinew
Length 14 cm

Although of typically Sioux construction and layout of beadwork lanes, these baby moccasins are unusual in their extensive use of black beads for the 'buffalo track' infill. The colors may have held some symbolic meaning for the maker. They may, alternatively, have been made for sale.

Child's moccasins, Eastern Plains, Eastern Sioux, circa 1880

Native leather, rawhide, glass beads, sinew, textile
Length 16 cm

Of slipper type construction, with integral tongues, these child's moccasins were probably made for sale by one of the Dakota groups. They are decorated with typical Eastern Sioux floral beadwork, employing a combination of 'lazy-stitch' and couched overlay techniques in extremely tiny 'cut' beads. The soles are made of thin rawhide. The ankles are edged with green cloth.

[Green, 1989]

Moccasins, Central Plains, southern Teton Sioux, circa 1890

Native leather, rawhide, glass beads, sinew
Length 23 cm

Moccasins with this style of floral decoration were made by the Sioux of Rosebud and Pine Ridge reservations in the 1890s, probably influenced by work produced by some of the Eastern Sioux groups. They are constructed of well-tanned cowhide, with rawhide soles, and beaded in 'lazy-stitch' technique. The designs consist of a symmetrical arrangement of trefoils and berries, flanked by 'feather' motifs.

Moccasins, Intermontane, Crow, 1920s

Native leather, rawhide, glass beads, cotton thread
Length 20.5 cm

These youth sized moccasins with rawhide soles are decorated with beaded stripes within a single lane-stitch perimeter lane comprising paired diagonals on a white background.

Moccasins, Northern Plains, Plains Cree, circa 1900

Canvas, native leather, glass beads, cotton thread, textile
Length 24 cm

These moccasins, formerly in the Herman Vonbank collection, are of slipper type construction, with fully-beaded canvas uppers and separate smoked hide soles. The couched overlay beadwork, with chevrons and other motifs composed of small rectangular blocks, within a border of green and blue beads, exemplifies the quality of work produced by the Plains Cree groups of Saskatchewan, Canada, much of which was produced for sale. The ankles are edged with a red cotton hemtape and a decorative edging of white beads. Each moccasin is lined with black silk.

Moccasins, Northern Plains or Plateau, circa 1900

Native leather, glass and metal beads, sinew, cotton thread
Length 23 cm

Constructed of thick, smoke-tanned moosehide, these moccasins are fully beaded in couched overlay technique with a symmetrical arrangement of stylized floral designs on a white background, sinew-threaded, cotton thread-couched. The 'dual side seam' construction may indicate a Plateau origin.

Moccasins, Plateau, possibly Nez Percé, circa 1890-1910

Native leather, glass beads, sinew
Length 24 cm

Of 'dual side seam' construction, this pair of heavily smoked hide moccasins is decorated with a bold floral composition in couched overlay technique. Floral and foliate designs composed of two colors—outline and infill—are typical of much Plateau beadwork from the late nineteenth and early twentieth century. Note the high ankle extensions. For a comparable pair, see Lanford, 1992: 40.

Moccasins, Northern Plains or Plateau, circa 1890
Native leather, glass beads, cotton fabric, cotton thread
Length 26 cm

Two quite different beadwork styles are combined on this pair of 'side seam' moccasins. The uppers are decorated with couched overlay beadwork comprising a bold diamond design with triangular appendages to three of the four points, within a modified lane-stitch border of diagonal stripes. The area to the inside of the ankle is beaded with stylized floral designs, also in couched overlay technique.

Northern Plains moccasins often employed a side seam construction. Careful examination of this pair, however, reveals a 'dual side seam' construction, as discussed by Dave Sager [1996], suggesting a possible Plateau provenance.

Together with a Cree floral-beaded shot pouch, these moccasins were collected by an ancestor of the wife of Major General H.M. Liardet, C.B.E., D.S.O., D.L. while serving in Canada in the early twentieth century. Both items were on display at the family home at Warningcamp House in Arundel, Sussex, until the contents of the house were sold at auction in 1993.

Made For Sale

Native American beadworkers were nothing if not inventive. When times were hard, they put their ingenuity to good use to produce a range of souvenirs and novelties that would appeal to early tourists. Many of the beaded articles they produced were inspired by store-bought prototypes.

Scissors case, marginal Plains, circa 1880 *(left)*
Native leather, glass beads, canvas, cotton fabric
Length 28 cm

This style of scissors case was a popular item made for sale by Indian groups of the marginal Canadian Plains. Large numbers were produced by the Plains Ojibwas and Saulteaux. The bold floral designs were directly influenced by floral styles shared with Ojibwa neighbors further to the east.

Pouch, marginal Plains, probably Saulteaux, circa 1900 *(right)*
Native leather, canvas, glass beads, velvet, cotton cloth
Length (excluding strap) 20 cm

This keyhole-shaped pouch, finely beaded with floral forms in couched overlay technique, is backed with smoked hide and edged with black velvet, with black velvet bows and handle. The bold floral designs and dark curvilinear stems are typical of beadwork from the marginal Plains region.

Holster, marginal Plains, possibly Saulteaux, circa 1870-80

Native leather, canvas, glass beads, woolen cloth
Length 23 cm

Indian-made novelties were in great demand in the late nineteenth century. Objects such as this holster were exhibited at the Colonial and Indian Exhibition, held in London in 1886, and typify both the nature of material sought by contemporary curio collectors and the ingenuity of Indian craft workers in producing objects that appealed to the Victorian sense of the exotic.

Belt set, marginal Plains, possibly Saulteaux, circa 1880-1900

Native leather, canvas, glass beads, cotton fabric
Length (belt) 101 cm, (holster) 20 cm, (knife sheath) 20 cm

This ensemble comprises matching floral-beaded belt, pistol holster and knife sheath. An identical set was exhibited at the Colonial and Indian Exhibition in London in 1886 and illustrated in a contemporary ladies' newspaper.
[Phillips, 1998: 216].

Wall bag, marginal Plains, probably Saulteaux, circa 1880-1900

Leather, canvas, glass beads, cotton cloth, wool yarn, cotton thread
Length 30 cm

This useful 'wall tidy' was probably made for sale by one of the Saulteaux groups of southwestern Manitoba. It is an Indian-made version of a popular novelty used in the Victorian home.

Bag, Northern Plains, possibly Plains Ojibwa, circa 1900

Native leather, glass beads, canvas, cotton cloth, cotton thread
Length (maximum) 46 cm

This bag, with its symmetrical composition of floral couched overlay beadwork within a colored border, is made of smoked moosehide, the oval panel beaded on canvas. Above the main beaded field is a panel of floral beadwork on a smoked hide ground.

Watch fobs, Southwestern Plains, Western Apache, circa 1900-20

Glass beads, cotton thread
Length 20 cm, 17.5 cm

Large numbers of loom-beaded watch fobs were made by the Western Apache groups, both for their own use as well as for sale. Many were beaded with geometric designs. The example on the left has a design of two deer; the one on the right a design apparently inspired by the 'Stars and Stripes'.

Apache bead loom kits were also popular among white Americans, and watch fobs of this kind would have been a relatively easy project for beginners.

[Ferg, 1987: 99; color plate 13]

Hatband, Southwestern Plains, probably Western Apache, circa 1920

Glass beads, cotton thread, horsehair
Length (doubled) 30 cm

Both loom-beading and horsehair weaving were produced by the Western Apache groups. This hatband incorporates both of these techniques – the narrow band is beaded with a greasy yellow background, each end joined by woven cords of braided dyed horsehair, with decorative horsehair tufts and glands. Some examples are made completely of woven horsehair. [Ferg, 1987: 102].

Beaded Tea Cosy, Northern Plains, circa 1930-50

Glass beads, canvas, cotton fabric
Height 20.5 cm, width 23 cm

This rather unusual example of souvenir beadwork was made by one of the Canadian Plains groups, probably either the Northern Assiniboine (Stoney) or the Plains Cree of Alberta or Saskatchewan. It was made for sale to support Native incomes, somewhere between the 1930s and about 1950.

Both front and back are decorated with solid couched overlay beadwork (spot stitch), on canvas. The designs consist of bold geometric designs, typical of the Canadian Plains groups. The units are made up of smaller square blocks, creating a checkered effect. This too is a common feature of beadwork from this area, and can be seen on shirt strips and many other articles of beadwork produced by the Stoneys and the Plains Cree.

Another classic Northern Plains feature of the design is the stacking of design units, as seen on the reverse side. This composition would not look out of place on a late nineteenth century Northern Plains beaded gun case.

Bead colors employed are opaque red, dark blue, pumpkin orange and translucent green, on a white background. Beads are of Czech stock, size 12/0, as favored by many Northern groups around this period.

Beaded novelties, Northern Plains, circa 1930-50

Glass beads, canvas, cotton cloth
Maximum length 19.5 cm

These items of beadwork were made for the souvenir market by the
Stoney-Assiniboine, Blackfoot or Plains Cree. Tourists to the Canadian provinces
eagerly sought items that were compact and easy to take home. The item at the top is
a beaded bracelet made in the shape of a wristwatch. The other items are napkin
rings, fully beaded in a style similar to the tea cosy on page 200.

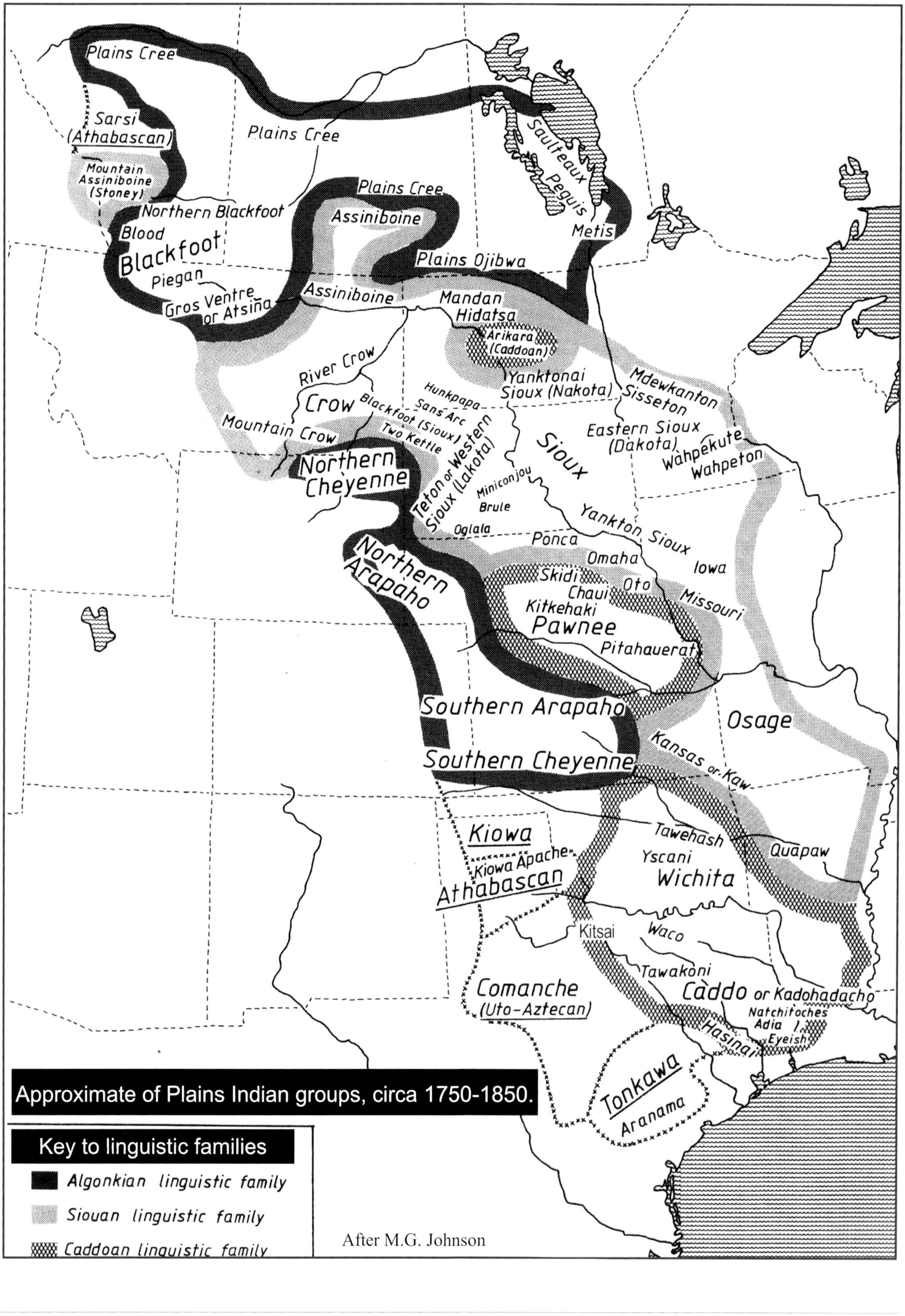
Plains Cree
Sarsi (Athabascan)
Plains Cree
Mountain Assiniboine (Stoney)
Plains Cree
Saulteaux Peguis
Northern Blackfoot
Assiniboine
Metis
Blood
Blackfoot
Plains Ojibwa
Piegan
Gros Ventre or Atsina
Assiniboine
Mandan
Hidatsa
Arikara (Caddoan)
River Crow
Yanktonai Sioux (Nakota)
Mdewkanton
Sisseton
Crow
Hunkpapa
Sans Arc
Blackfoot (Sioux)
Two Kettle
Mountain Crow
Eastern Sioux (Dakota)
Wahpekute
Wahpeton
Northern Cheyenne
Teton or Western Sioux (Lakota)
Sioux
Miniconjou
Brule
Oglala
Yankton Sioux
Northern Arapaho
Ponca
Omaha
Iowa
Skidi
Chaui
Oto
Kitkehaki
Missouri
Pawnee
Pitahauerat
Southern Arapaho
Osage
Southern Cheyenne
Kansas or Kaw
Kiowa
Kiowa Apache
Athabascan
Tawehash
Yscani
Wichita
Quapaw
Kitsai
Waco
Tawakoni
Comanche (Uto-Aztecan)
Caddo or Kadohadacho
Natchitoches
Adia
Eyeish
Hasinai
Tonkawa
Aranama
Key to linguistic families
Algonkian linguistic family
Siouan linguistic family
Caddoan linguistic family
After M.G. Johnson
Approximate of Plains Indian groups, circa 1750-1850.

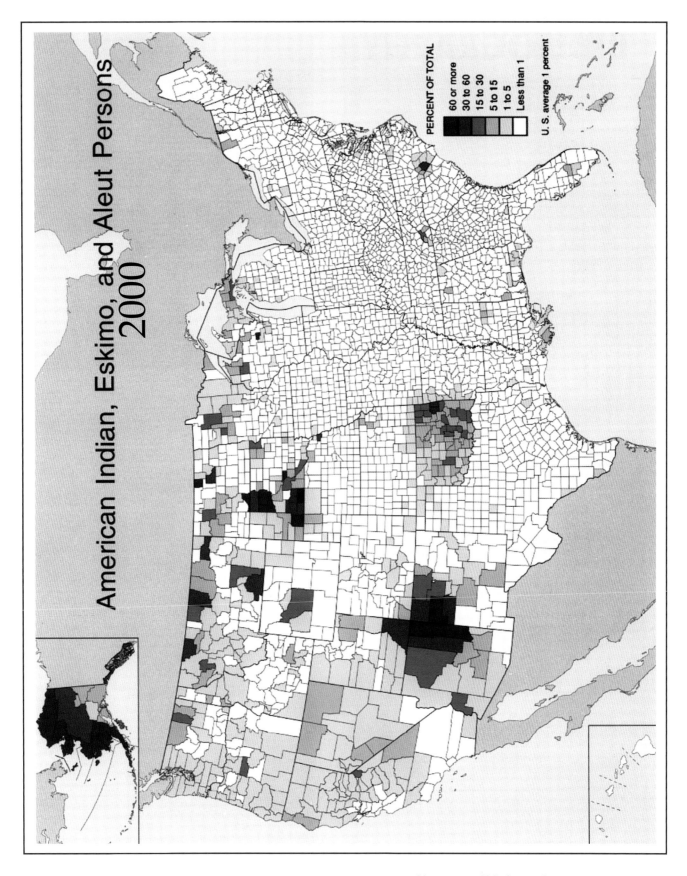

American Indian, Eskimo, and Aleut Persons
2000

PERCENT OF TOTAL

60 or more
30 to 60
15 to 30
5 to 15
1 to 5
Less than 1

U. S. average 1 percent

Map courtesy U.S. Census Bureau

A Warrior I Have Been

BIBLIOGRAPHY

Behold These Things

Dempsey, Hugh A. *Tribal Honors – A History of the Kainai Chieftainship*. Alberta: Alberta Historical Resources Foundation, 1997.

Ewers, John C. *Blackfeet Crafts*. Lawrence, Kansas: Haskell Institute; Department of the Interior, 1945.

Green, Richard. "A Northern Plains Loop Necklace." *Whispering Wind* 16:2 (1983).

Hungry Wolf, Adolf and Beverly. *Blackfoot Craftworker's Handbook*. Invermere, British Columbia: Good Medicine Books, 1977.

Scriver, Bob. *The Blackfeet – Artists of the Northern Plains: The Scriver Collection of Blackfeet Indian Artifacts and Related Objects, 1894-1990*. Kansas City: Lowell Press, Inc.,1990.

Stepney, Philip H. R. and David J. Goa. (ed.) *The Scriver Blackfoot Collection: Repatriation of Canada's Heritage*. Edmonton: Provincial Museum of Alberta, 1990.

Taylor, Colin F. and Hugh Dempsey. *With Eagle Tail – Arnold Lupson and 30 Years among the Sarcee, Blackfoot and Stoney*. London: Salamander Books Ltd, 1999.

Something Splendid I Wear

Conn, Richard. "Blackfeet Women's Clothing." *Whispering Wind* 17.3-5 (1984).

Conn, Richard. *Robes of White Shell and Sunrise, Personal Decorative Arts of the Native American*. Denver: Denver Art Museum, 1975.

Corey, Carolyn. *The Tradecloth Handbook*. St. Ignatius: Méti Mercantile Press, 2001.

Ewers, John C. *Blackfeet Crafts*. Lawrence, Kansas: Haskell Institute; Department of the Interior, 1945.

Green, Richard. "Iroquois Beaded Whimsies." *Bead Society of Great Britain newsletter* 58 (May 2001): 11-15.

– "Trade Cloth Dresses." *Bead Society of Great Britain newsletter* 69 (September 2003).

– "Trade Cloth Dresses – Part 2." *Bead Society of Great Britain newsletter* 70 (December 2003).

Hail, Barbara A. *Hau, Kola! – The Plains Indian Collection of the Haffenreffer Museum of Anthropology*. Rhode Island: Brown University,1980.

Hungry Wolf, Adolf and Bevery. *Blackfoot Craftworker's Book*. Invermere, British Columbia: Good Medicine Books, 1977.

Morris, Carole. "Bead Tile Mats." *Bead Society of Great Britain newsletter* 66 (December 2002).

Penney, David *Art of the American Indian Frontier – The Chandler-Pohrt Collection*, Detroit Institute of Arts, 1992.

Scriver, Bob. *The Blackfeet – Artists of the Northern Plains*. Kansas City: Lowell Press, 1990.

Stepney, Philip H.R. and David J. Goa (ed.). *The Scriver Blackfoot Collection: Repatriation of Canada's Heritage*. Provincial Museum of Alberta, 1990.

In Paint and Feathers

Cunningham, Tom. *The Diamond's Ace – Scotland and the Native Americans*. London and Edinburgh: Mainstream Publishing, 2001.

Gallop, Alan. *Buffalo Bill's British Wild West*, Stroud: Sutton Publishing, 2001.

Some Honor I Seek

Hathaway, Nancy. *Native American Portraits, 1862-1918*. San Francisco: Chronicle Books, 1990.

Phelps, Stephen. *Art and Artefacts of the Pacific, Africa and the Americas – The James Hooper Collection*. London: Hutchinson & Co. Ltd., 1975.

White Man's Vision

Brown, Robert. *The World: Its Cities and Peoples, Vol.5*. London, Paris and Melbourne: Cassell & Company Limited, n.d.

Catalog

Brown, Joseph Epes. *The Sacred Pipe – Black Elk's Account of the Seven Rites of the Oglala Sioux*. Norman: University of Oklahoma Press, 1953.

Christie's. *Important American Indian Art*, 29 November 1995, New York.

Ewers, John C. *Blackfeet Crafts*. Lawrence, Kansas: Haskell Institute; Department of the Interior, 1945.

Ferg, Alan (ed.) *Western Apache Material Culture – The Goodwin and Guenther Collections*. Tucson: University of Arizona Press, 1987.

Green, Richard. "A Northern Plains Loop Necklace." Whispering Wind 16:2 (Summer 1983).

– "Eastern Sioux and Red River Métis Beadwork." *Whispering Wind* 22:1 (Spring 1989).

– "Cheyenne Cradle Covers." *Whispering Wind* 23:3 (Summer/Fall 1990).

– "Teton Sioux Style Vests, circa 1890-1910." *Whispering Wind* 26:3 (Nov / Dec 1993).

– "Sioux Fully-Beaded Yoke Dresses." *Whispering Wind 28:4 (1997).*

– "An Aspect of Design Irregularity in Teton Sioux Beadwork." **Whispering Wind 28:5** (1997).

– "Apache Beaded Bags." *Bead Society of Great Britain newsletter* 59 (July 2001): 16-17. (Archived on BSGB website, 2003).

– "An Unusual Style of Northern Plains Belt Set." *Whispering Wind* 31:5 (2001).

– "Central Plains Saddle Blankets." *Whispering Wind* 32:6 (2002).

– "Late 19th Century Western Apache Miniature Cradles." *Whispering Wind* 33:3 (2003).

Hail, Barbara A. *Hau, Kola! – The Plains Indian Collection of the Haffenreffer Museum of Anthropology.* Rhode Island: Brown University, 1980.

Herbst, Toby and Joel Kopp. *The Flag in American Indian Art*. New York State Historical Association / University of Washington Press, 1993.

Kilgour, Ruth Edwards. *A Pageant of Hats*. New York: Robert M McBride Co, 1958.

Kroeber, Alfred L. *The Arapaho*. New York: American Museum of Natural History, 1902.

Lanford, Benson. "Beaded Moccasins of the Plateau Tribes." *Fibre Arts: The Magazine of Textiles* 19:3 (Nov. / Dec. 1992) 40-43.

Mails, Thomas E. *The People Called Apache. New Jersey:* Englewood Cliffs, 1974.

Mason, Otis T. *Cradles of the Native Americans.* Washington: Smithsonian Institution Annual Report, 1887 (reprint available).

Peterson, Harold L. *American Indian Tomahawks*. New York: Museum of the American Indian, Heye Foundation,1965.

Phelps, Stephen. *Art and Artefacts of the Pacific, Africa and the Americas - The James Hooper Collection*. London: Hutchinson & Co Ltd, 1975.

Phillips, Ruth B. *Trading Identities – The Souvenir in Native American Art from the Northeast, 1700-1900*. Seattle: University of Washington Press, 1998.

Sager, Dave. "The Dual Side Seam: An Overlooked Moccasin." *American Indian Art 21:2 (Spring 1996).*

Scriver, Bob. *The Blackfeet – Artists of the Northern Plains*. Kansas City: Lowell Press Inc, 1990.

Stewart, Tyrone. "Cheyenne Moccasins." *American Indian Craft and Culture* 5:9 (1971).

Taylor, Colin F. (ed.) *The Native Americans – The Indigenous People of North America*. London: Salamander, 1991.

Torrence, Gaylord. *The American Indian Parfleche – A Tradition of Abstract Painting*. Seattle: University of Washington Press / Des Moines Art Center, 1994.

Vestal, Stanley. *Sitting Bull, Champion of the Sioux*. Norman: University of Oklahoma Press, 1957.

Wissler, Clark. *Decorative Art of the Sioux Indians*. New York: *Bulletin of the American Museum of Natural History*, Vol.XVIII, 1904.

– *Some Protective Designs of the Dakota*. New York*: Anthropological Papers of the American Museum of Natural History, Vol.I, Part II*, 1907.

Wooley, David (ed.) *Eye of the Angel – The Derby Collection*. Northampton, Massachusetts: White Star Press, Northampton, Massachusetts, 1990.

Wroth, William. (ed.) *Ute Indian Arts & Culture – From Prehistory to the New Millennium.* Chapter by Craig D. Bates. Colorado Spings: Colorado Springs Fine Art Center, 2000.

Pow wow culture is constantly evolving. This young
'traditional' dancer at United Tribes Pow Wow, Bismarck,
North Dakota, leads the way into Native American future.
Photograph by Jonathan Smith

I guess what really gets me is when people assume that we've 'lost our traditional ways', because they see that we don't live that romanticized version of what it is to be Native. I always tell people that tradition is not a static concept. It's beautiful the way that our culture and spirituality is timeless — it is just as relevant today as it was for our ancestors. All our prophets' teachings are just as appropriate now as they were then, and I believe that they will be so for our children and grandchildren, no matter what comes.

- Nico Strange Owl, Northern Cheyenne